MW01147934

THE AMERICAN WAR
IN VIETNAM

Recent titles in
Contributions in Military Studies
Series Advisor: Colin Gray

THE AMERICAN WAR IN VIETNAM

LESSONS, LEGACIES, AND IMPLICATIONS FOR FUTURE CONFLICTS

Edited by
LAWRENCE E. GRINTER
and
PETER M. DUNN

CONTRIBUTIONS IN MILITARY STUDIES, NUMBER 67
Greenwood Press
New York
Westport, Connecticut
London

Library of Congress Cataloging-in-Publication Data

The American war in Vietnam.

(Contributions in military studies, ISSN 0883-6884 ;
no. 67)
    Bibliography: p.
    Includes index.
    1. Vietnamese Conflict, 1961-1975—United States.
2. United States—History—1961-1969.   3. United
States—History—1969-   . I. Grinter, Lawrence E.
II. Dunn, Peter M.   III. Series.
DS558.A45   1987   959.704'33'73   87-11856
ISBN 0-313-25759-0 (lib. bdg. : alk. paper)

Library of Congress Catalog Card Number: 87-11856
ISBN: 0-313-25759-0
ISSN: 0883-6884

First published in 1987

Greenwood Press, Inc.
88 Post Road West, Westport, Connecticut 06881

Printed in the United States of America

The paper used in this book complies with the
Permanent Paper Standard issued by the National
Information Standards Organization (Z39.48-1984).

10 9 8 7 6 5 4 3 2 1

Copyright Acknowledgements

The editors and publisher gratefully wish to acknowledge permission to use material
from the following works:

Carl von Clausewitz, *On War*, ed. and trans. by Michael Howard and Peter Paret.
Copyright © 1976 by Princeton University Press. By permission of Princeton University Press.

John D. Waghelstein, "Post-Vietnam Counterinsurgency Doctrine" from the *Military
Review* Vol. 65, No. 5, © May 1985. By permission of the editor.

Lawrence E. Grinter, "How They Lost: Doctrine, Strategies and Outcomes of the
Vietnam War" from the *Asian Survey*, Vol. 15, No. 12, © December 1975. By permission of the Regents of the University of California.

Harry Summers, "A Strategic Perception of the Vietnam War" from *Parameters* ©
June 1983. By permission of the editor.

Contents

Abbreviations

ARVN	Army of the Republic of Vietnam
ASD/ISA	Assistant Secretary of Defense for International Security Affairs
Associated States	French IndoChina until 1954 (Vietnam, Laos, and Cambodia)
CINCPAC	Commander in Chief, Pacific
COIN/LIC	Counterinsurgency and Low-intensity Conflict
CORDS	Civil Operations and Revolutionary Development Support
COSVN	Central Office for South Vietnam (Hanois' field command in South Vietnam)
DRV (DRVN)	Democratic Republic of Vietnam
GVN	Government of Vietnam
LIC	Low-intensity Conflict
MACV	Military Assistance Command, Vietnam
MTT	Mobile Training Team
NLF (NLFSV)	National Liberation Front (of South Vietnam)
NVA	North Vietnamese Army (same as PAVN)
PAVN	People's Army of Vietnam
PME	Professional Military Education
RVN	Republic of Vietnam
RVNAF	Republic of Vietnam Armed Forces
SAF	Special Action Force
SAR	Search and Rescue
SEAL	Sea-air-land team

SOCs	Special Operations Commands
USACGSC	United States Army Command and General Staff College
Viet Cong	The insurgent forces in South Vietnam
WSOs	Weapons Systems Officers

Preface

The American war in Vietnam was the first major military commitment made by the United States in which we failed. Understanding why we failed is the purpose of this volume. The book looks at four critical factors that bore on U.S. conduct in Vietnam: how the war was perceived, how it was fought, whether different strategies would have succeeded, and what the war's legacy is for future U.S. conflict performance.

The origin of this volume stems from two panels on the Vietnam War at the twenty-fifth annual meeting of the Southeast Conference Association for Asian Studies held at North Carolina State Univeristy, Raleigh, January 16–18, 1986. The panelists included Joe Dunn, Peter Dunn, Noel Eggleston, Lawrence Grinter, Alan Gropman, Nguyen Hung, Earl Tilford, and John Waghelstein. The panelists agreed to revise their papers and assemble them into a book format. Lawrence Grinter and Peter Dunn volunteered to coedit the volume. In addition, Joe Dunn agreed to write the book's analytical introduction and Harry Summers was contacted for a contribution. Thus the book's contributors constitute both military officers and scholars. All but one contributor participated in the Vietnam War.

The coeditors wish to thank the fine contributions of the individual authors and the highly professional work of Mildred Vasan, Maureen Melino, Nick Allison, Trish Lorange Taylor, and others at the Greenwood Press. Both editors and contributors hope that this volume will make a further contribution to understanding the American experience in the Vietnam War and that it will better equip our country to deal with the conflicts of the future in which the United States may be involved.

1

INTRODUCTION AND OVERVIEW

A dozen years after the communist takeover of South Vietnam, there is growing agreement in American military and academic circles that U.S. power in Vietnam was misapplied. But there is very little agreement on the nature of the challenge the United States confronted in Vietnam, or on how—if U.S. power had been applied differently—it should have been applied. Moreover, since South Vietnam came under Hanoi's domination, a veritable siege of insurgency, guerrilla wars, and low-intensity conflicts has laid hold of the Third World. Thus, understanding what the United States did in Vietnam and why it went wrong remains a critical prelude to understanding how our subsequent and future interventions will fare.

In his analysis of the growing literature and debate on the American role and strategy in Vietnam, Dr. Joe P. Dunn surveys the rich field of literature, histories, reports, and conferences that have burgeoned, including Col. Harry Summers' widely debated *On Strategy: The Vietnam War in Context*. Dunn then places this new book in the context of the debate.

1

Joe P. Dunn

On Legacies and Lessons: The Literature and the Debate

The search for lessons dominates the historiography of the Vietnam War. No part of the vast extant literature is more important than that which deals with how the war was fought and what can be learned from the experience. Defining and digesting the lessons of any war is an enterprise that should be approached with proper caution, and certainly this truth applies to Vietnam. During this long war, the United States applied too many lessons from previous conflicts in situations that were not analogous. But the quest for legacies and lessons is imperative.

Many scholarly conferences in recent years have debated the relevant lessons of the Vietnam experience. The edited collections of the papers and discussions of four conferences devoted exclusively to the war are particularly interesting: Peter Braestrup's *Vietnam As History: Ten Years After the Paris Peace Accords* (1984), from a Woodrow Wilson International Center conference; Harrison E. Salisbury's *Vietnam Reconsidered: Lessons from a War* (1984), from a heralded four-day conference at the University of Southern California; Harry A. Wilmer and James F. Veninga's *Vietnam in Remission* (1985), from a conference in Texas; and John Schlight's *The Second Indochina War Symposium* (1986), from a conference sponsored by the U.S. Army Center on Military History. The following chapters in this book come from panels devoted to strategies, lessons, and legacies of the war at the Southeast Conference Association for Asian Studies held in Raleigh, North Carolina, January 16–18, 1986. These essays demonstrate a diversity of views on the military and political lessons of the war and on the implications for future low-intensity conflicts.

The debate over American strategy in Vietnam has a long history. During the early advisory years, American reporters in Vietnam, military advisors like the legendary John Paul Vann, and members of the Joint Chiefs of Staff all criticized aspects of our policy and operations. As the United States assumed the major combat role in 1965, criticism of strategy grew. Air Force Chief of Staff General Curtis LeMay was one of the early bitter critics of American restraint as he preached strategic bombing of the North. At the height of the war, General William Westmoreland and Admiral U. S. Grant Sharp indicated some of their frustrations with policy in their *Report on the War in Vietnam* (1969). In the immediate postwar years, both senior officers wrote memoirs that more thoroughly developed their criticisms of the policy and strategy limitations under which they operated. Westmoreland's *A Soldier Reports* (1976) and Sharp's *Strategy for Defeat* (1978) echoed themes expressed by other's in volumes such as Marine Corps General Lewis W. Walt's *Strange War, Strange Strategy* (1970), Marine Corps Colonel William Corson's *The Betrayal* (1968) and *The Consequences of Failure* (1974), and Army General Dave Richard Palmer's popular history, *Summons of the Trumpet: A History of the Vietnam War from a Military Man's Viewpoint* (1978).

General Douglas Kinnard's *The War Managers* (1977), the result of a survey of the 173 General Officers who served in Vietnam between 1965 and 1972, offered a panorama of dissent over how the war was conducted. W. Scott Thompson and Donaldson D. Frizzell's *The Lessons of Vietnam* (1977) excerpted from a conference on "The Military Lessons of Vietnam" the assessments of senior military officers, civilian policymakers, and academics. Providing illuminating insight from our allies are Stephen T. Hosmer, *et al.*, *The Fall of South Vietnam* (1980), a collection of the perspectives of senior Vietnamese military and civilian leaders on the failures of American strategy; General Nguyen Cao Ky's *How We Lost the Vietnam War* (originally titled *Twenty Years and Twenty Days*) (1976); General Tran Van Don's *Our Endless War: Inside Vietnam* (1979); and Cao Van Vien and Dong Van Khuyen's *Reflections on the Vietnam War* (1980).

The best civilian academic critiques of American strategy include Robert W. Komer's *Bureaucracy Does Its Thing* (1972) and *Bureaucracy at War: U. S. Performance in the Vietnam Conflict* (1986); Robert L. Gallucci's *Neither War Nor Peace: The Politics of American Military Policy in Vietnam* (1975); Douglas Blaufarb's *The Counter-Insurgency Era: U. S. Doctrine and Performance* (1977); Herbert Y. Schandler's *The Unmaking of a President: Lyndon Johnson and Vietnam* (1977); Guenter Lewy's monumental *America in Vietnam* (1978); Leslie H. Gelb and Richard K. Betts' *The Irony of Vietnam: The System Worked* (1979), a classic on the functioning of bureaucratic policy-making; James C. Thompson's *Rolling Thunder: Understanding Policy and Program Failure* (1980); and Wallace G. Thies' *When Governments Collide: Coercion and Diplomacy in the Vietnam Conflict, 1964–1968* (1980).

On a related subject, at the end of the war, a spate of books emerged on the purported breakdown of the U. S. military in Vietnam. Examples included Richard Boyle's *The Flower of the Dragon: The Breakdown of the U. S. Army in Vietnam* (1972), William L. Hauser's *America's Army in Crisis* (1973), Zeb B. Bradford and Frederic J. Brown's *The United States Army in Transition*

(1973), Richard Gabriel and Paul Savage's *Crisis in Command* (1978), and Cecil B. Currey (using the pseudonym Cincinnatus), *Self-Destruction: The Disintegration and Decay of the United States Army During the Vietnam Era* (1981).

Although a large literature on American strategy and performance in Vietnam existed, it was Colonel Harry G. Summers, Jr., U.S. Army, who raised the level of discourse. Summers served as an infantry squad leader in Korea and as a battalion and corps operations officer in Vietnam. As a negotiator with the communist forces at the end of the war, he was one of the last Americans to leave Saigon in the final days. After the war, with senior Army staff concurrence, Colonel Summers undertook a critical analysis of the failure in Vietnam. The result was *On Strategy: The Vietnam War in Context* (1981 by the Army War College). A call to return to the classic principles of war as articulated by the great early nineteenth-century Prussian strategist Karl von Clausewitz in his seminal eight volume work *On War*, Summers's book received critical acclaim, and the colonel became somewhat of a national celebrity. (An article by Colonel Summers, which surveys some of the main arguments in *On Strategy*, is reprinted as one of the readings in this book.)

Despite high praise for *On Strategy* from a broad range of reviewers, the number of critics and the substantive level of their critiques are growing. For some, the prime issue is Summers's seemingly cavalier dismissal of the revolutionary nature of the war, the Viet Cong, and the counterinsurgency effort. Others are concerned by his depreciation of the political constraints that limited U.S. strategic options and his hindsight certainty about issues such as what China would have done. The most damning commentators question Summers's very understanding of Clausewitz and the relevance of Clausewitzian dictates to the specific circumstances in Vietnam. Allan R. Millett, one of the first to challenge Colonel Summers sharply, offers what remains one of the most devastating evaluations. Millett accuses Summers of missing the point, of naïveté and facile understanding of Clausewitz and intellectual error. Professor Millett, a Marine Corps Reserve Colonel and one of the nation's most eminent military historians, branded *On Strategy* an eccentric polemic that could be ignored had it not attracted such institutional endorsement within Army circles.[1] Finally, the book could have been better organized and written. Summers has a tendency to proclaim rather than prove his points; a dogmatic tone is evident at times.

So why has *On Strategy* had such impact? Because, whatever its failings, the book has many virtues. Colonel Summers rose above the more superficial "revisionist" interpretations of U.S. failures in Vietnam represented in books such as Norman Podhoretz's *Why We Were in Vietnam* (1982) and Richard Nixon's *No More Vietnams* (1985) that tended to concentrate blame on Congress, the media, the antiwar movement, liberals, and academia. While these factors may have played a role, Summers insists that the causes are much deeper. Like other revisionists, Summers believes that the war was honorable and winnable; and he condemns the hesitant, vacillating civilian leadership exhibited by the McNamara coterie and Lyndon Johnson. But at core were the failures of military leadership. Summers denounces the military's acceptance of the "management mentality," failure to do the necessary preintervention strategic planning, reluctance of the Joint Chiefs of Staff to stand up courageously against pernicious directions, and General Westmoreland's ill-conceived, improvisational war strategy.

Colonel Summers touched a wide spectrum of war critics, and he appealed to the predilections and prejudices of many. He understood war through experience and the study of military history rather than through management theory. Whether *On Strategy* becomes a classic or has its brief moment and fades is not so important as the catalytic role it has played. It spurred thought and debate, and it continues to do so. One enthusiastic, early reviewer proclaimed that *On Strategy* would "make history." In many ways it has. But had not Summers taken pen in hand, General Bruce Palmer's *The 25-Year War: America's Military Role in Vietnam* (1984) probably would have assumed the role played by *On Strategy*. The two authors influenced each other, and their books make similar points.[2]

Other excellent recent "revisionist" studies of American military strategy include George C. Herring's "American Strategy in Vietnam: The Postwar Debate," *Military Affairs* (April 1982), Stanley L. Stanton's *The Rise and Fall of an American Army: U. S. Ground Forces in Vietnam* (1985), Thomas C. Thayer's *War Without Fronts: The American Experience in Vietnam* (1986), and the aforenoted Robert W. Komer's *Bureaucracy at War* and John Schlight's edited compendium *The Second Indochina War Symposium*.

A brief word should be said about Timothy J. Lomperis's *The War Everyone Lost—And Won; America's Intervention in Vietnam's Twin Struggles* (1984), which raises provocative questions about the nature of the war and American strategy.[3] Lomperis argues that the war needs to be understood as two-dimensional. It was a thirty-year struggle for national legitimacy between the successive South Vietnamese governments and the communists. And, in larger context, the war tested the efficacy of the enemy's revolutionary strategy of protracted peoples' war. Lomperis explains that the battlefield failure of the heralded Tet 1968 uprising forced the communists to abandon their highly touted revolutionary strategy. After 1968, the war became primarily a conventional assault of the North upon the South—which ultimately the North Vietnamese won; however, the United States had denied the North Vietnamese political legitimacy, and the concept of a peoples' war of national liberation suffered a grievous setback.

If we do not understand the Vietnamese communists today, it is not for a lack of scholarship. The multitudinous literature on the topic includes names such as George Tanham, Paul Mus, John T. McAlister, Dennis Duncanson, P. J. Honey, Robert Turner, David G. Marr, William Duiker, William S. Turley, and Huynh Kim Khanh and Bernard B. Fall, not to mention the doyen of Vietnamese studies. Works more specifically on the insurrection include Michale Charles Conley's *The Communist Insurgency Infrastructure in South Vietnam* (1968), Frances Fitzgerald's highly acclaimed but superficial and deeply flawed *Fire in the Lake:*

The Vietnamese and the Americans in Vietnam (1972), and Paul Berman's *Revolutionary Organization: Institution-Building Within the Peoples Liberation Armed Forces* (1974) are introductions to the Viet Cong. Douglas Pike's classic works *Viet Cong* (1966), *War, Peace, and the Viet Cong* (1969), *The Viet Cong Strategy of Terror* (1970), *History of the Vietnamese Community Party* (1978), and his *PAVN: The People's Army of Vietnam* (1985) are the most definitive sources available. William Darryl Henderson's *Why the Viet Cong Fought* (1979) is useful. Harvey Meyerson's *Vinh Long* (1970), Jeffrey Race's *War Comes to Long An* (1972), William R. Andrews' *The Village War* (1973), and James W. Trullinger, Jr.'s *Village at War* (1980) are helpful microcosmic studies of how the Viet Cong operated in the villages. F. J. West's *The Village* (1972) and John L. Cook's *The Advisor* (1973) are memoirs by military advisors who attempted to counteract the guerillas at the local level. Stuart A. Herrington's *Silence Was a Weapon: The Vietnam War in the Villages* (1982) demonstrates how the Phoenix program in the early 1970s virtually eliminated the Viet Cong in Hau Nghia province.

Finally, the enemy speaks for himself. The North Vietnamese today freely admit that truth was not their greatest virtue during the war. Defense Minister Vo Nguyen Giap gives a candid version of North Vietnamese goals in *Unforgettable Days and Months* (1975), *How We Won the War* (1973), and with Van Tien Dung, *The Great Spring Victory* (1977); PAVN General Tran Van Tra's *History of the B–2 Front* (1982) was so outspoken that he got into trouble with his superiors; and Le Duan's *Letters to the South* (1985, in Vietnamese) removes any doubt that the North organized, controlled, and ran the National Liberation Front (NLF) from the first. Two leading NLF figures tell their stories in Nguyen Thi Dinh's *No Other Roads to Take* (1976) and Truong Nhu Tang's *A Viet Cong Memoir* (1985), the latter a remarkably valuable book by a disillusioned former high NLF official.

The testimony of the boat people eloquently attests to the painful tragedy of life in the South today under the North Vietnamese. The reality of the suffering has caused some former antiwar activists to reassess their earlier arrogance, but others cling to the myth that accounts are exaggerated and life is actually better now than under previous South Vietnamese regimes. A few of the more systematic renderings of life under the communists include Nguyen Ngoc Ngan's *The Will of Heaven* (1981); Nguyen Long and Harry H. Kendall's *After Saigon Fell: Daily Life Under the Vietnamese Communists* (1982); Stephen Morris's "Vietnam Under Communism," *Commentary* (September 1982); Nguyen Ngoc Huy's *Vietnam Under Communist Rule* (1982) and his later, more global *A New Strategy to Defend the Free World Against Communist Expansion* (1983); Stephen Denney and Ginetta Sagan's *Violations of Human Rights in the Socialist Republic of Vietnam, April 30, 1975–April 30, 1983* (1983); Jacqueline Desbarats and Karl D. Jackson's "Vietnam 1975–1982: The Cruel Peace," *The Washington Quarterly* (Fall 1985); and former NLF sympathizer Doan Van Toai and David Chanoff's *The Vietnamese Gulag* (1986).

SURVEY OF THIS BOOK'S CHAPTERS

All but one of the authors of this volume participated in the Vietnam War. Five are senior military officers; four are academics. Although independently written without knowledge of the other contributors or a preconceived theme, the similarities and insights, and the implicit debate are remarkable. All the chapters reflect the more tempered tones of current Vietnam War scholarship, and three questions predominate: What was the nature of the war—revolutionary peoples' war or conventional conflict? Was the war winnable? What, if anything, could have been done differently to achieve military and political success? All the authors address Harry Summers' views directly or indirectly. This collection, like the war that spawned it, demonstrates the difficulty in reaching consensus on the legacies of the war.

Nguyen Hung's introductory essay explains how the most prominent theories about the war have been disproven by events or how they are otherwise incomplete explanations. As he points out, the war meant different things to various Americans and Vietnamese. But for the communist leaders, who initiated and sought to control the revolutionary movement from the beginning, the ultimate goal was a complete socialist transformation of South Vietnam through class struggle and violence. Nationalism and independence from Western influence, which engendered wide popular appeal, were merely intermediate stages. Many in the NLF, who had been led to believe otherwise, learned the bitter truth after 1975. Fundamental to Hung's argument is his judgment on the root cause of the war: Despite the foreign pressures and involvements, the war's origins came from within Vietnamese society and produced the showdown between conflicting visions of the revolution's end result—a liberal, pluralistic society or a totalitarian, socialist one. Hung concludes by noting that although communist organization and tactics appear effective instruments for gaining power in the Third World, the societies they have produced show little regard for liberty or economic well-being. He argues that if the United States intends to perform as a global power to help nurture a world order consistent with our interests and values, then America bears certain responsibilities to weak and threatened countries. But meeting these responsibilities requires consensus about what we want to do, how much and how long we are willing to commit. American strategy in future conflicts will depend on the answers to these important questions.

Lawrence Grinter articulates his position emphatically: Our minimal objective in South Vietnam could have been achieved, but political failures and misplaced priorities on both sides of the Pacific spelled defeat. Despite inflated rhetoric, billions of dollars, and tens of thousands of American lives, three successive American presidents were unwilling to pay the political costs to achieve success. Our military strategy was constrained by self-imposed political restraints that restricted our bombing policy, limited the ground war to South Vietnam, and our strategy relied inordinately upon firepower, often employed indiscriminately, inside South Vietnam. These realities led us to pursue a hapless and costly defensive strategy of attrition, which allowed Hanoi to control the tempo of the war and ultimately brought the North to victory. After the 1973 Paris accords, the United States was even less willing to maintain the economic and political costs necessary to sustain South Vietnam.

The United States, however, did not bear all the responsibility for failure. Grinter explains that at the most basic level, the war was a revolutionary struggle between two Vietnamese political systems. To succeed, South Vietnam needed to solve its internal problems and develop a legitimate political order that would involve its citizens in their own defense and national welfare; however, South Vietnam failed to provide the necessary political alternative to the communists and was thus increasingly vulnerable. Grinter concludes that a better-led South Vietnam, defended by a more rational military strategy, could have survived the threats against it. Not only were the political necessities not achieved, Grinter laments that they were never even seriously addressed.

Air Force Colonel Alan Gropman agrees that the war was winnable; however, like Summers, he views it as a conventional conflict and does not concern himself with the political dynamics of South Vietnam. For Gropman, the problem centered in the Washington bureaucracy's failure to understand the nature of war and the decisive capabilities of air power when properly employed. He castigates Lyndon Johnson, Robert McNamara, John McNaughton, and others who succumbed to exaggerated fears of China, the Soviet Union, and protests against the bombing. Overriding the consistent advice of the Joint Chiefs of Staff, the civilian leaders focused upon the peripheries rather than on what should have been the key target. Gropman maintains that the question of whether the war was counterinsurgent or conventional was ultimately irrelevant because the strategy should have been the same in either case—take the war to the heart of North Vietnam and eliminate Hanoi as a factor in the conflict.

In his fine history of the use of air power during the various stages of the war, Gropman brands *Rolling Thunder* a farce in conception and implementation, and he alleges that even *Linebacker I* and *II*, while great tactical achievements, fell short of the full capabilities of strategic bombing. In January 1973, with North Vietnam defenseless against total destruction, the U.S. allowed Hanoi to grasp a peace very favorable to them. Colonel Gropman concludes that the U.S. "misapplied air power from one end of the war to the other," and his essay is one of the most articulate and forceful advocacies in print of strategic air power.

Another Air Force officer, Major Earl Tilford, also offers an insightful assessment of air power during the war but with a very different interpretation than Colonel Gropman. Both men agree on the general failure of U.S. air strategy and particularly upon the uselessness of *Rolling Thunder*, but then they part company. Gropman asserts that the United States failed to employ fully the awesome technology at its disposal. Tilford counters that the problem was the overreliance upon technology rather than the development of a sound strategy consistent with the realities of the situation. Tilford rejects Gropman's and Summers's views of the war as strictly conventional, and he is clearly less sanguine about what could have been accomplished by less restrained air power. In fact, Major Tilford contends that the primary problem with *Rolling Thunder* was that it attempted to employ conventional means against the North to deal with an unconventional revolutionary threat in the South. He disputes Gropman's argument that even if the war were defined as counterinsurgency, the ability of North Vietnam to support the forces in the South could have been eliminated. Tilford explains that the Viet Cong and PAVN fighting in the South needed relatively small amounts of daily supplies, many of which came across Cambodia, and even unrestrained bombing could not have completely cut off the flow. He also challenges the air power enthusiasts' credo, as well expressed by Gropman, that *Linebacker II*–type bombing at an early state in the war was possible and would have produced results equivalent to those witnessed in December 1972.

Tilford concludes where he began—that the Air Force is tending to explain its failure to achieve its goals in Vietnam by looking for easy answers such as the kind that Colonel Gropman provides; moreover, the service prefers to define the war as an aberration little related to what it will face in the future. Tilford brands this the same hubris that underlay so many of our failures in Vietnam.

Colonel Harry Summers's short essay in this book, "A Strategic Perception of the Vietnam War," summarizes many of his central points from *On Strategy*. Arguing that North Vietnam used the Viet Cong insurgency as a "smoke screen" to hide its true intentions, Summers believes the United States was deceived about the real nature of the war; moreover, the United States had no clear objective in Vietnam and could not formulate viable, precise, and consistent strategy. In Summers's view, faulty strategic thinking led to faulty military operations in the field. We did not apply enough force with enough effect against the real enemy's "center of gravity"—North Vietnam's army, territory, and, if need be, capital. Instead, the United States saw the war as revolutionary when it was conventional, and saw the Viet Cong guerrillas rather than North Vietnam's regular army as the center of gravity. The alternative strategic implication of Colonel Summers's indictment is this: With the President and Congress in agreement, we should have struck North Vietnam with overwhelming military force.

Of all who have praised or damned Harry Summers's *On Strategy*, Peter Dunn offers one of the most interesting critiques. Dunn accepts Vo Nguyen Giap's, Van Tieng Dung's, and other North Vietnamese generals' assessments of the war as primarily a revolutionary conflict; and given the history and circumstances that the United States inherited, he questions whether victory in any meaningful sense was possible. Specifically on Summers, Dunn implies that the author of *On Strategy* has a simplistic understanding of Clausewitz, an understanding that leads Summers to espouse rigid and doctrinaire principles of war. Dunn points out that Clausewitz's views were still developing at the time of his early death, and that Clausewitz himself warned against taking his evolving thought as gospel. Moreover, the Prussian theorist drew his lessons exclusively from European masters such as Machiavelli, and the set pieces of Frederick the Great and Napoleon. Clausewitz had almost nothing to say about insurgency, even though the term "guerrilla warfare" comes from the Spanish resistance against Napoleon's occupying army. In sum, both modern Asian insurgency on terrain quite foreign to the nineteenth-century European battlefield and the dynamics of contemporary American democratic politics are elements far afield from Clausewitz's experience. Dunn asserts that had Clausewitz been an American general in charge of U. S. strategy in Vietnam, he probably would have lost the war.

If Clausewitz may not be totally pertinent, Colonel Dunn offers a theorist more relevant to understanding our adversaries and the nature of the war in Vietnam. This is the famous fourth-century B.C. Chinese strategist, Sun Tzu, author of *The Art of War* and intellectual godfather for Mao Zedong and Vo Nguyen Giap. Drawing upon Sun Tzu and the history of warfare in China and Indochina, Dunn details why he believes that Summers's proposed actions—an invasion of North Vietnam, for example—would not have been successful. Dunn explains that it is not necessary to speculate about what it would have been like to encounter the mass resistance of the North Vietnamese populace, even discounting the possibility of Chinese intervention, since a real example exists. In their incursion into North Vietnam in the spring of 1979, the Chinese confronted extensive local resistance and withdrew without meeting the main Vietnamese forces.

Peter Dunn's argument is no less subject to criticism than is Summers. In fact, Summers has addressed the relevance of Sun Tzu and reaffirmed his own emphasis upon the universality of Clausewitz in a recent article.[4] Peter Dunn's thoughtful assessment remains provocative nevertheless.

Noel Eggleston also confronts Summers. Like Grinter and Hung, he views the problem in Vietnam as more political than military; and like Tilford and Peter Dunn, he questions whether the war was actually winnable. Eggleston sides with an impressive list of scholars who stress the revolutionary nature of the conflict, and he challenges Summers's depreciation of the Viet Cong and counterinsurgency. He notes that the colonel would have a stronger case if he accepted for example, Timothy Lomperis's explanation of the change in the nature of the war in 1968 or Pike's concept of *dau trinh* (Vietnamese for struggle). More importantly, Eggleston faults Summers for his counterfactual determinations that a declaration of war and full war footing were possible in 1965; that the likelihood of Chinese intervention or Soviet response were so minimal as to be of no concern; and that Lyndon Johnson had the political options to conduct the war as Summers would have liked at earlier stages. Finally, Eggleston doubts that any level of American military power could have broken North Vietnam's will and determination and brought victory.

The next chapter differs significantly from the rest, but it too addresses, at least by inference, some of the same questions as the others. A Latin American expert and Vietnam veteran, Colonel John Waghelstein, Commanding Officer of the 7th Special Forces, calls for a more serious commitment to counterinsurgency and low-intensity conflict today. While Harry Summers excoriates the overemphasis upon counterinsurgency in Vietnam, Waghelstein insists that the

U.S. Army was never really serious about counterinsurgency when it was "forced" upon them in the early 1960s, and that after the war they dismissed the concept. Summers claims that counterinsurgency did not work; Waghelstein, like Grinter, that it was never really tried. In his advice for the future, Waghelstein explains that the insurgent challenge cannot be met exclusively, or even predominantly, by military means. But the military should inculcate these lessons from Vietnam: work within the capability and systems of the host country; stick to basic assistance rather than quick fixes of high technology, logistics, and firepower, which can overwhelm less developed nations; think small and long-term; and know the language and culture of the country in which you operate. Thus Waghelstein stands more with Grinter, Tilford, Dunn, and Eggleston than with Summers and Gropman.

In the coeditors' concluding chapter to the book, Peter Dunn and Lawrence Grinter compare and contrast the various authors' views on several critical strategy questions, then step back from the essays to comment on the broader societal and philosophical aspects of the American war in Vietnam. Vietnam's legacy for future low-intensity conflict behavior by the United States completes the book.

NOTES

1. Colonel Allan R. Millett, book review in *Marine Corps Gazette* (August 1982), pp. 75–76.

2. For the most thorough comparative treatment of these two books, see Gary R. Hess, The Military Perspective on Strategy in Vietnam: Harry G. Summers, Jr., *On Strategy: A Critical Analysis of the Vietnam War* (Novato, CA, 1982); Bruce Palmer, Jr., *The 25-Year War: America's Military Role in Vietnam* (Lexington, KY, 1984). *Diplomatic History* vol. X no. 1 (Winter 1986), pp. 91–106.

3. Lomperis was a commentator for one of the sessions from which this volume of papers came. Other participants not represented in the book included Paul Kattenburg, John Gates, John Garver, and Paul Godwin.

4. Colonel Harry G. Summers, Jr., "Clausewitz: Eastern and Western Approaches to War," *Air University Review* (March-April 1986), pp. 62–71.

II

HOW THE WAR WAS PERCEIVED

There is a basic concept in psychology that says motivation conditions perception. The Vietnam War proved something of the reverse: Perceptions, whether voluntarily chosen or forced on people, influence behavior. The Vietnam War was many things to many people. It was a war of national liberation, and a war against communist aggression. It was a war to end all guerrilla wars, and a war to save a country. It was alternately seen as a just war, an immoral war, a war against foreign imperialism, a war in defense of a country's freedom. These were the stereotypes, the shortcuts, that in the passion and emotion of the war were substituted for more logical analysis about what was actually happening in Vietnam and what should be done.

In his essay, Professor Nguyen M. Hung surveys the most prominent theories about the nature of the Vietnam War, and he concludes with his own views. Dr. Hung identifies four prominent "theories" about the Vietnam War: the civil war thesis; the anticolonialist theory; the cold war/domino theory; and the view of the war as an extension of the French Indochina War. At its core, however, Dr. Hung believes the Vietnam War was a struggle between Vietnamese patriots to determine the final destiny of the Vietnamese revolution. The theories Dr. Hung analyzes are important; they swept along millions of peoples' emotions and viewpoints, and they influenced their decisions. They also figured in the selection of strategies and how the war was fought by the combatants.

Clearly American confusion about the war's nature added up to a strategic failure in its own right. We violated Karl von Clausewitz's foremost principle. In *On War*, the early nineteenth-century strategist stated:

> The first, the supreme, the most far-reaching act of judgment that the statesman and commander have to make is to establish . . . the kind of war on which they are embarking; neither mistaking it for, or trying to turn it into, something alien to its nature.

The Vietnam War in Retrospect: Its Nature and Some Lessons

The Vietnam War directly affected the lives of over three million Americans who went through the war and many more millions of Vietnamese on both sides of the conflict. It has left a deep impression on over one million Vietnamese refugees scattered around the world. In the United States, the "Vietnam syndrome" has affected both American veterans and Vietnamese refugees, and it has haunted the American public and leadership for years.[1] In policy debates, one often heard allusions to the "lessons of Vietnam." It is difficult, however, to draw lessons of Vietnam without a clear understanding of the nature of the Vietnam War. During the war years (1959–75), discussion over the nature of the Vietnam War and its policy implications was often driven by emotion and ideological bias rather than by reason and insight. The immediacy of the war and the lack of hindsight propelled many people into hasty conclusions and faulty judgments. Twelve years have now passed since the fall of Saigon, and fourteen years since the last American troops left South Vietnam. With the benefit of historical hindsight and new evidence that has come out since the end of the war, it seems the right time to review the most prominent theories about the war's nature and see what lessons might be drawn. Those theories were critical because they influenced millions of people's ideas about the war's nature and character, and they also affected the choice of competing strategies and responses, for better or worse.

THEORIES OF THE WAR'S NATURE

The "Civil War" Thesis versus Postwar Communist Admissions

In the 1960s, George Kahin and John Lewis advanced a theory that was widely accepted within U.S. antiwar circles. These authors maintained that the Vietnam

War was basically a civil war, a war that pitted the South Vietnamese people against the repressive Ngo Dinh Diem regime and its successors in Saigon. According to this theory, the struggle against the Diem regime was started by "former Southern Vietminh," Hanoi at first disapproving of their actions but later forced to go along with them.[2] The implications of this theory are that United States involvement in Vietnam was both illegal (because it interfered in a civil war) and reactionary (because it supported anti-democratic forces). This theory is now thoroughly discredited by the public admissions of Vietnamese communist authorities and by revelations and complaints of disillusioned cadres of the National Liberation Front of South Vietnam (NLFSV) and members of the "Third Forces" in South Vietnam.[3] Doan Van Toai, one of the disillusioned, admitted that he was duped and "hypnotized by the political programs of the NLF."[4] Truong Nhu Tang, a former Minister of Justice in the Provisional Government of South Vietnam and a leading member of the NLFSV, bitterly complained that the war in South Vietnam was controlled and directed from beginning to end by the Lao Dong (now Vietnamese Communist) Party. Nguyen Khac Vien, the Vietnamese Communist historian was quoted as saying: "The Provisional Revolutionary Government was always a group emanating from the Democratic Republic of Vietnam (DRV). If we [the DRV] had pretended otherwise for such a long period, it was because during the war we were not obliged to unveil our cards."[5] Vo Bam, a North Vietnamese general, proudly told a French television crew in 1983, "On May 19, 1959, I had the privilege of being designated by the Vietnamese Communist Party . . . to unleash a military attack on the South to liberate the South and reunify the father land."[6] It is now apparent that reunification of Vietnam under communist control, rather than some idealistic struggle against authoritarianism, was always the primary goal of the communist leaderships and it is impossible to deny the fact that the people in South Vietnam enjoy much less freedom now under communist rule than they did at any time under the "repressive" regimes of the previous South Vietnamese governments.

The "Anticolonialist" Theory

Another theory, which is also shared by many American historians and antiwar writers, views the Vietnam War as an anticolonialist war and the end of the war in 1975 as a victory of nationalism over imperialism. This theory pictures the Vietnamese communists as the champions of Vietnam's independence, the United States as aggressor, and simply dismisses those Vietnamese who fought against the communists as collaborators or imperialists. According to Frances FitzGerald, "The NLF, after all, pursued a peasant revolution designed to take power from the hands of the foreigners and the few Vietnamese—landlords and officials—who profited from their rule."[7] The fall of Saigon at first seemed to validate this theory and prompted some historians to revise their previous positions. For example, Joseph Buttinger, who in the 1950s was an admirer of Ngo Dinh Diem and his brand of nationalism, came out with a new book in 1977 in which he

downgraded the whole Diem experience and revised his interpretation of Vietnamese history by claiming, erroneously, that "the whole of Vietnam had become
communist by the end of World War II."[8]

Such a theory simply cannot be squared with the facts. First, if the war in
Vietnam were an anticolonialist war, it should have started in 1964 at the time
the United States began to send combat troops to Vietnam, or even in 1962
when the United States started to increase the number of American advisors in
South Vietnam, rather than in 1959 when there were almost no Americans in
South Vietnam (and certainly fewer than there are Soviet advisors in Vietnam
today). Second, proponents of the anticolonialist thesis must prove that the
primary objectives of United States policy in Vietnam were territorial aggran-
dizement and/or economic exploitation. This has not ever been convincingly
proven or even argued. Third, this theory seems to contradict the previous one,
which holds that the war in Vietnam represented a struggle against Diem's authoritarianism and repression. One possible way to reconcile these two theories is
to show that Diem was an American lackey or, as the 1983 Public Broadcasting
System series on "Vietnam: A Television History" put it, Diem was an "American Mandarin." Diem, of course was far from being an American puppet, and it
would be intellectually dishonest to label him anything less than a Vietnamese
nationalist.[9] If the war was simply a struggle of nationalists and imperialists, then
how would one account for the fact that the struggle against the present communist regime still goes on within and outside Vietnam in spite of the fact that "independence" had been gained and the American "imperialists" have long
departed?

The "Cold War" Theory and the Domino Theory

Opposed to these theories is one that views the Vietnam War as part of the
cold war and the struggle between the "free world" and the communist world,
between freedom and totalitarianism; and further that failure to contain com-
munism in South Vietnam would lead to communist expansion in the rest of
Southeast Asia. This theory could explain the involvement of foreign powers in
the Vietnam War (the United States, Australia, New Zealand, Thailand, the
Republic of Korea, and the Philippines on the side of South Vietnam; and the
Soviet Union and the People's Republic of China on the side of North Vietnam).
This thesis was first expounded by the U.S. Secretary of State, then by Presidents
Eisenhower and Kennedy, and was generally accepted by the American leaders
and people between 1961 and 1966–67. It remained plausible to American
"hawks" and the old anticommunist hands in Vietnam, as well as to younger
people who grew up in South Vietnam during and after the formation of the
First Republic, and especially to those who stayed behind in Vietnam in 1975
and have been deprived of whatever precious freedom they previously enjoyed.[10]
Critics of this theory complained about the naïveté of cold-war rhetoric. People
who were concerned with ideology questioned the democratic claim on the

anticommunist regimes in South Vietnam. Those who were concerned with power politics questioned the strategic significance of South Vietnam and the validity of the domino theory.

Actually, what has happened in Southeast Asia since the fall of Saigon in April 1975 neither proves nor disproves the domino theory. Although the communists have not succeeded in toppling governments in Southeast Asia, they, nevertheless, have gained control of all three Indochinese states. Besides, the domino theory had its origins in Europe, and became prominent in the mid–50s when the communist world still seemed a monolithic bloc and the Vietnamese communists were riding high on their victory at Dien Bien Phu. Thus it was not intended for the mid–70s when the old communist alliance was in disarray and other Southeast Asian nations by then had been able to benefit for 20 years from the American shield, to consolidate themselves and learn from the lessons of Vietnam. For the ideologues who criticized America's allies in South Vietnam and supported North Vietnam and the NLFSV for their moral rectitude, it is probably time to reconsider their position in light of the compelling evidence about the totalitarian nature of the regime set up by the "liberators" of South Vietnam.[11]

The War as an Extension of the French Indochina War

Still another theory views the Vietnam War, also called the Second Indochina War, as a natural consequence of the French Indochina War, which lasted from 1946 to 1954. According to the proponents of this theory, the Geneva Accords of July 1954 which ended the First Indochina War and partitioned Vietnam at the seventeenth parallel, only provided for a cease-fire between the combatants but failed to reach a final solution of the complex political aspects of the conflict in Vietnam. Conflict among Vietnamese parties and the issue of national reunification were supposedly to be solved within two years through negotiations and elections under international guarantees. When, as a result of Diem's objections, negotiations and elections failed to take place, war inevitably occurred. This theory may explain why the Second Indochina War happened, but it falls short of addressing the question about the nature and genesis of the political conflict in Vietnam.[12]

Vietnamese communist leaders who initiated and controlled the armed struggle against the successive regimes in South Vietnam were essentially straightforward and consistent in their analysis of the nature of the war. To them, the Vietnamese conflict was basically a struggle between socioeconomic classes. Vietnam was a country in continuous revolution whose final destiny was communism. The war in South Vietnam was only the initial stage of a two-stage revolution, a "national revolution" preceeding a "socialist transformation" of South Vietnam.[13] Hence, independence from Western influence was a necessary precondition to the final goal, not an end in itself. Since Vietnamese communists used nationalism for other purposes, they must be seen as the champions of class struggle rather than of nationalism and "national reconciliation," as a few adherents and supporters of the National Liberation Front of South Vietnam wanted to believe.[14] It was only natural that those who joined or supported the NLFSV in the sincere belief that they were working to liberate the people of South Vietnam from political oppression and foreign domination and to achieve "national reconciliation" were in for a big disappointment. Such were the cases of Truong Nhu Tang, Doan Van Toai, Chau Tam Luan, Nguyen Cong Hoan and others.[15]

WHY SOUTH VIETNAM FELL: THE ROOT CAUSE

Thus the war in Vietnam meant different things to different people. People and governments on both sides of the conflict fought and opposed the war for different reasons. Cold war politics and big power rivalry were integral parts of the war. But they were *aggravating factors rather than the root causes* of the conflict. One simply cannot dismiss the motivations of the Vietnamese participants themselves regarding the war in their country. The search for independence has always been an important goal of the Vietnamese revolution, but the real cause of the Vietnam conflict was deeply rooted in disagreements over its final destiny among Vietnamese revolutionaries. The demand for modernization and radical change in the socio-political-economic order was articulated early in the twentieth century when Vietnamese patriots began debating how to cope with French colonialism and improve the conditions of the country.[16] In the 1930s and 1940s, although all Vietnamese anticolonialist parties, including the Indochinese Communist Party, agreed on the goal of national independence, there was no consensus on the vision of a postindependence political order. Disagreement clearly existed between the Indochinese Communist Party and other nationalist parties that opposed the former's narrow position on revolution, religion, and its own role in the anticolonialist struggle. Within the communist ranks there also was disagreement between the Stalinists and the Trotskyites who were disturbed by the Soviet purges.[17]

There is no question that the history of Vietnam is the history of long struggles against foreign domination, but it is equally important to recognize that the effort in Vietnam also has been a battle *between Vietnamese patriots*. In the twentieth century this conflict was most typified by those who on the one hand believed in the possibility of harmonious relations between social classes and the respect for basic individual freedoms in an independent Vietnam, and on the other by those who believed in class conflict and the dictatorship of the proletariat. This internal strife went on concurrently with the effort to regain national independence from the French. It continued long before the landing of American combat troops in South Vietnam in 1964, and it continued after the departure of American troops in 1973, and after the fall of Saigon in 1975. The collapse of South Vietnam did not represent the triumph of nationalism over imperialism as much as it did the triumph of totalitarianism and the failure of the quest for human dignity in Vietnam.

THE DEBATE OVER STRATEGIES AND TACTICS

From a military point of view, few would disagree that the war in Vietnam was, or at least began as, an unconventional war fought within a revolutionary context, and that it was a multifaceted war fought on many fronts—military, political, economic, and social. But there was no consensus about what lessons could be drawn from it or how to cope with a war of such complexity. Military strategists and political analysts were divided between those who believed the war could not be won and those who believed it could be won or at least did not have to be lost; between those who thought that Vietnam was predominantly a political struggle and those who maintained that, at least following the assassination of President Diem, it was largely a conventional military conflict.

Civilian analysts such as William Duiker, John McAllister, Guenter Lewy, Russell Weigley, and Lawrence Grinter viewed the war as a political struggle, a revolutionary war[18] against which a "conventional bureaucratic-military response to revolutionary warfare [did] not work."[19] Duiker implied the war could not be won because of the "contrast between the chronic weakness and political ineptitude of the Saigon governing elite and the political genius of the Communist Party," and he maintained that the failure of the United States to provide adequate military support was "not a decisive factor" in the defeat[20]. Grinter did not think the final outcome was inevitable; he believed that defeat could have been avoided had the Thieu government been given more time, guaranteed continuing American military and economic assistance, and Hanoi punished for its violations of the 1973 Paris peace accords.[21] President Nixon even went further and asserted that the United States had won the military war in South Vietnam by 1973 and blamed the Congress and the press for abandoning South Vietnam when the communists subsequently violated the Paris peace agreements.[22]

The majority of military analysts believed the war could have been won or at least should not have been lost if it had been handled differently. They believed the war was lost not because of overreliance on military strategy but because of excessive political control by civilians over military operations. They complained of the "overintellectualization" of the Vietnam War, a military campaign fought and controlled to the smallest details by politicians or their appointees who were concerned with gains and losses in Washington rather than by commanders in the field. Admiral Ulysses G. Sharp wrote of the frustration of having to fight a war with "one hand tied behind our backs."[23] General William Westmoreland lamented the political constraints on attacking communist sanctuaries adjacent to South Vietnam.[24] Colonel Alan L. Gropman berated the "humiliating, exceptionally expensive, and probably unnecessary American defeat" because American political leaders "squandered and misapplied" air power against secondary targets in the southern part of North Vietnam.[25] Colonel Harry Summers accused the American political leadership not only of misperception of the nature of the war, which, following the assassination of President Diem, had become a conventional war, but also of failure to come up with a strategy for success.

pour additional troops and war material into South Vietnam, the latter was handicapped by dwindling American aid and the lack of American air support to interdict Hanoi's supply lines. General John E. Murray graphically described the way the United States abandoned its South Vietnamese ally:

At the height of American power over there, we had 433 U.S. and allied combat battalions; the enemy had 60 (larger) combat regiments. In 1974 when we had pulled out, the ARVN had 189 battalions, and the enemy had built up to 110 regiments. There was a 40 percent decrease in allied ground firepower. Take away the B–52s, take away the F–4s, and take away U.S. naval gunfire— take all that away. Then we started to support the South Vietnamese with two percent of the money we had used to support our own U.S. forces in Vietnam against a lesser enemy

—Salisbury, *Vietnam Reconsidered*, p. 143.

General Van Tien Dung, the North Vietnamese Army's Chief of Staff, who led the final assault on South Vietnam, analyzed the impact of the cut of American aid on the "balances of forces which was advantageous to the revolution" in South Vietnam as follows:

The decrease in American aid had made it impossible for Saigon troops to carry out their combat and force-deployment plans. In the 1972–1973 fiscal year the Americans had given their protégés $1,614 million in American aid. In fiscal year 1973–1974 it was only $1,026 million, and in fiscal year 1974–1975 it fell to $700 million. Nguyen Van Thieu had to call on his troops to switch to a 'poorman's war': . . . [their] fire support fell nearly 60 percent because of the shortage of bombs and shells; mobility also decreased 50 percent because of a shortage of aircraft, vehicles, and even fuel.

—Van Tien Dung, *Our Great Spring Victory: An Account of the Liberation of South Vietnam* (New York and London: Monthly Review Press, 1977), pp. 17–18.

  31. See Lewy, *America*; Westmoreland, *Soldier's Report*; and Nixon, *Real War*.

III

HOW THE WAR WAS FOUGHT

With so many competing theories and perceptions about the Vietnam War's nature, it is not surprising that there was little agreement in the United States among the public or in government about what was happening inside and to South Vietnam. Was the war caused by North Vietnamese aggression or by South Vietnamese corruption? Was it a civil war or an international war? Revolutionary or conventional? If you cannot agree on causes and character, how can you develop a coherent response?

Which brings us to the problem of U.S. objectives. In June 1944, General Dwight D. Eisenhower's orders read, "You will enter the continent of Europe and, in conjunction with other United Nations, undertake operations aimed at the heart of Germany and the destruction of her armed forces." The objectives were clearly defined, and the military and political aims of the United States meshed well with what Professor Russell F. Weigley has described as "the American way of war."

For a century prior to the commitment of American forces to Vietnam, the United States' wars generally had been crusades in which the might of industry was wedded to the rectitude of morality; however, American objectives were never clearly defined in Vietnam, and a multiplicity of rationales were offered. At best, we seemed to have two basic objectives: (1) how to "create conditions" in which an anticommunist government could survive in South Vietnam; and (2) how to make North Vietnam pay for its aggression. But according to surveys by retired Brigadier General Douglas Kinnard, 70 percent of the U.S. Army generals who served in Vietnam were unsure of our reason for being there. Indeed, our objectives seemed to change over time. Following the 1968 Tet offensive, the United States opted for a "no win" policy in Vietnam. As the Vietnamization program continued, "peace with honor" became our expressed goal.

Did confusion as to goals and objectives doom the Republic of Vietnam despite what happened—or might have happened—on the battlefields of South Vietnam and in the air war over the North? The chapters that follow by Lawrence Grinter, Alan Gropman, and Earl Tilford discuss the political and military aspects of both the ground war and the air war. The authors prompt the reader to think through the issues and problems raised.

Did the failure to define the goals and the conventional nature of our military response translate into ineptitude in the prosecution of the war? In concentrating on the fighting inside South Vietnam and on the nature of the Saigon governments, Dr. Lawrence E. Grinter proposes three irreducible political requirements for an allied victory and then analyzes how the foundations of those requirements crumbled, bringing on failure. Was there a military solution outside of South Vietnam that related to the complex political issues between Hanoi, Saigon, Washington, Moscow, and Peking? Colonel Alan L. Gropman, a retired Air Force officer, maintains that American air power, if used properly, could have changed the final outcome of the war. According to Colonel Gropman, despite impressive air power performance at the siege of Khe Sanh in 1968, in response to the North Vietnamese invasion of the spring of 1972, and the eleven-day bombing of North Vietnam in December 1972, "airpower was misapplied from one end of the war to the other." While agreeing that air power was misapplied, Major Earl H. Tilford, Jr., another Air Force officer, challenges Colonel Gropman's thesis. Major Tilford asserts that traditional concepts of air power were inappropriate in the unconventional context of the Vietnam War. He argues that the institutional problems within the Air Force led it to use air power outside the structures of a rationally constructed strategy.

3

Lawrence E. Grinter

Vietnam: The Cost of Ignoring the Political Requirements

United States policy failed, and South Vietnam and the United States failed to win the Second Indochina War for three fundamental reasons:

—Under pressure from the North Vietnamese/Viet Cong totalitarian assault, South Vietnam failed to develop both a self-sustaining national defense and an effective, legitimate political system.

—Allied forces were unable to destroy enough communist forces inside South Vietnam or to bring enough pressure against the North Vietnamese heartland to force a basic change in Hanoi's policy.

—The United States failed to adequately sustain its support of South Vietnam in 1974 and 1975, while Moscow and Beijing were prepared to support Hanoi indefinitely.

Thus, the irreducible *political* requirements of an allied victory in Vietnam were:

—a multidimensional strategy in South Vietnam, based on both population protection and territorial security, which built a popular and enlarging political community linking Saigon to the people while also defending the country

—an allied decision to take the war out of South Vietnam either through a U.S. supported, South Vietnamese invasion of the sanctuaries and North Vietnam, and/or the equivalent of the *Linebacker I* and *II* bombing campaigns in 1966 or 1967

—United States congressional and executive support for South Vietnam for however long it took to help that country defend itself

All three requirements of victory in Vietnam were fundamentally political. In each case—South Vietnam's defense and development, the need for an early strategic South Vietnamese/American attack on what became the major source of the aggression, North Vietnam, and the necessity for indefinite U.S. support of South Vietnam—the requirements presumed fundamental, long-term political foundations that either were not forthcoming or that disintegrated. These realities do not discredit the heroic defense of the Republic of Vietnam by South Vietnamese and American forces, or the two allies' goal of preventing a totalitarian country from destroying a comparatively free country. The cause was just. The goal was moral. But ultimately the long years of defending the republic against its ruthless adversary gradually wore down South Vietnamese and American morale until, in the spring of 1975, the war effort suddenly collapsed and Saigon surrendered to Hanoi's Soviet tanks.

That the war could have had a different outcome is the question that this chapter explores. The war was lost not due to lack of material resources or human courage. It was lost because the necessary *political* requirements in South Vietnam, and between Saigon and Washington, could not be brought to bear. Those facts need not lead anyone to "stab-in-the-back" or "what-might-have-been" accusations or indulgences. Clausewitz teaches that war is fundamentally a political enterprise. And as Michael Howard writes: "Wars are not tactical exercises writ large. They are, as Marxist military analysts quite rightly insist, conflicts of societies, and they can be fully understood only if one understands the nature of the society fighting them."[1] The Second Indochina War pitted very different societies against each other. That a government that cruelly tramples on human freedom eventually won neither justifies its motives nor discredits the freedom that was fought for by South Vietnam, by the United States, and by the fifteen other countries that aided the Republic of Vietnam.

SOUTH VIETNAM'S DILEMMAS

Few countries in recent history have been subjected to such severe strain and endured as valiantly as South Vietnam. The Republic of Vietnam's (RVN) citizens were hardworking, intelligent, and courageous, as they proved again when so many came to U.S. shores in the last decade. The governments and social structure of South Vietnam between 1961 and 1975 were typical of many Third World societies, although in Vietnam these derived their special qualities from traditional Confucian-elitist origins and practices under Vietnamese (and Chinese) Mandarin concepts of authority. What greeted Americans when they encountered Vietnam in 1961 was the end result of centuries of Vietnamese, and then French colonial practices: A class and caste system perpetuated after independence in 1954 by a series of political and military leaders—Diem, Minh, Khanh, Ky, and Thieu. Naturally there were inequities, repression, and arbitrary arrests. But compared to the policies of North Vietnam (the Democratic Republic of Vietnam, or DRVN) under Ho Chi Minh and his lieutenants, who simply liquidated or expelled those people they found objectionable, life in South Vietnam was much freer. Of course, with the American intervention came enormous U.S. military and logistical spending and disturbances in South Vietnam, which added to the inequities of the country's wealth and social structure. Under wartime circumstances a huge black market flourished, which perpetuated the privileges of the elite and entrepreneurial classes and, after 1964, drew senior military officers and their wives into the spoils.

The communist attack on South Vietnam employed Ho Chi Minh's strategy of revolutionary warfare, which was borrowed from Lenin's and Mao's "organizational weapon" approach to political mobilization.[2] The Vietnamese Communist party began with a strategic view of revolution as a stage-by-stage *social process* aimed at preempting the government's contact with the people and motivating between five and ten times more manpower at local levels through indoctrination, social control, and the redistribution of power, status, and wealth. Carefully adapting to and championing local grievances and issues, the clandestine insurgent organization threw a net of social, political, economic, and military associations around the people. This social mobilization and organization-building approach emphasized the participation, voluntary or coerced, of peasants, laborers, and soldiers into the party's programs. Strategically it was multidimensional and Marxian; revolution was seen as an unfolding process of social and class conflict. Victory would come when a decisive superiority in the overall balance of forces, achieved through mass organizational work that dramatized (and sometimes rectified) grievances, had been accomplished.[3] The use of terror was controlled, selective, and prevalent. The communists seldom diverged from this basic approach except to vary the military pressure.

It remains a subject of sharp debate whether it was the communists' organizational capabilities, the causes they championed, their comprehensive view of revolution, or all of these, which gave the communist insurrection such momentum. Knowledgeable analysts of the movement have debated the interplay of "indigenous" and "imported" factors in the National Liberation Front of South Vietnam (NLFSV). Others, studying communist recruitment patterns, found various motives for joining the movement: abuses suffered at the hands of the French or Saigon, desire for more land, nationalism, the social mobility of a career in the Viet Cong.[4] But the sheer effectiveness of the Vietnamese communists' use of social-organizational-military force cannot be doubted.

As Samuel Huntington commented:

Only the communists have consistently demonstrated the ability to organize and structure [political] participation and thus to create new institutions of political order. Not revolution and the destruction of established institutions, but organization and the creation of new political institutions are the peculiar contributions of communist movements to modern politics. The political function of communism is not to overthrow authority but to fill the vacuum of authority.

Huntington continued:

North Korea and North Vietnam early achieved a level of political development and political stability which was long absent in South Korea and still longer absent from South Vietnam. . . . The difference between north and south in both countries was not the difference between dictatorship and democracy but rather the difference between well organized, broadly based, complex political systems, on the one hand, and unstable, fractured, narrowly based personalistic regimes, on the other.[5]

However, the Saigon governments did not combat communist revolutionary warfare with a counter-organizational strategy until late in the game. Instead their doctrine of political authority, typified by the Ngo Dinh Diem regime and also evident in some of Nguyen Van Thieu's practices, was rooted in traditional Vietnamese and Chinese concepts of government. Mandarins saw the purpose of government to be the maximization of the central authorities' influence. Power was concentrated among the elites. At the level of the masses, the key to success lay in maintaining stable behavior through techniques of social control. Diem believed that the central authorities would enjoy a "Mandate of Heaven" if they set a personally moral example. His brother Nhu, however, relied more on coercion.[6] Thieu and Ky believed they could retain American support if they set up Western-style political institutions. In actual practice, however, the Vietnamese at the top acted as though the key to power lay in manipulating rivals, not in morality or democracy. Competitors were neutralized, sometimes eliminated. Deception was the mark of effectiveness. The use of force expected. As Douglas Pike described it in terms that applied to *both* Saigon and Hanoi:

The world of organizational infighting is fluid and dynamic, in constant flux. One must keep running simply to hold his own. . . . The world should never know precisely where one stands. . . . The best leader is paternalistic, sly, skilled at intrigue, master of the deceptive move, possessor of untold layers of duplicity, highly effective in the world in which he moves. Sagacity in the follower consists in knowing whom to join and when, for timing is all important. It is no accident that the Vietnamese hold the professional magician in particular awe.[7]

Government, then, was designed to "keep people from endless scheming about life and calculations about how to improve one's lot. Good government should train people to keep their stations and to accept the structure of society."[8] After 1964, South Vietnam's military oligarchy prospered without the need to draw support—political or economic—from the country's peasant and labor ranks. As the huge U.S. military intervention transformed the country, the republic's most fatal political flaw appeared: the country's wartime leadership did not have to rely on the people to stay in power, nor did it have to fight the communists on their terms, nor even confront their strategy. The oligarchy was protected.

Of course the structure of South Vietnamese society shifted with the impact of the war—drafting millions of young men into the armed services, moving them about the country, and sacrificing them in the nation's defense. And the multifaceted challenge that Hanoi and the Viet Cong posed to the RVN—in the villages, at the province levels, and from the main force units—also forced changes in the Thieu government's approach. After the Tet 1968 communist offensive, the Saigon government moved to protect *both* people and territory. An emergency decentralization of the armed forces, police, and administrative apparatus occurred. By late 1969 there were about two million South Vietnamese in the People's Self-Defense Forces and about 400,000 arms had been issued. Accelerated pacification campaigns were underway, and by mid–1969 the GVN, with U.S. support, was concentrating on maintaining sustained local security, attacking the communist infrastructure, and reinvigorating the villages and land reform programs.[9] But even as the GVN Central Pacification and Development Council, backed by MACV's Office of Civil Operations and Revolutionary Development Support (called CORDS), made real progress between 1969 and 1971, whenever major fighting erupted, these programs reverted to emergency cleanup efforts and refugee welfare schemes. They were heavily damaged when the North Vietnamese struck again in March 1972.

Hanoi seriously underestimated the vigor of the American and South Vietnamese reaction to its 1972 offensive. By that summer, with the exception of the terrible An Loc siege, the communist attack had petered out. In the first two months of the aggression, conservative U.S. estimates indicated the communists had lost one-third of the total men committed: 20,000 dead and 40,000 wounded.[10] President Nixon ordered the mining of North Vietnam's harbors, and U.S. aircraft employing laser-guided bombs were able to stop 70 to 80 percent of the war material coming into the South. The air attack on North Vietnam also seriously hurt the country's hydroelectric industry and rail complex. But GVN losses of secure population also were serious; in the Mekong Delta they were 15 percent. The NVA controlled South Vietnam's border districts in Tay Ninh, Phuoc Long, and Binh Dinh provinces. All of Quang Tri was lost. Large security gaps were also left in Quang Tin, Quang Nam, and Thua Thien provinces.[11] By late 1972, the overall population security picture showed a serious deterioration of conditions for over 20 percent of South Vietnam's people.

Thus, year after grinding year it was South Vietnam, not North Vietnam, that bore the brunt of the fighting and the resulting U.S./GVN conventional military reaction. In spite of horrendous communist manpower losses, Hanoi could play the game on the comparative cheap, remaining on the strategic offensive against the allies, while U.S./GVN ground operations stayed confined to South Vietnam with the minor exceptions of the Cambodian invasion of May 1970 and the Lam Son 719 operation into Laos in February 1971. Moreover, the enormous volume of allied artillery shells and air operations against targets inside South Vietnam contributed to a traumatic population shift between 1965 and 1973. Perhaps one-fifth of the RVN's population moved, the country changing from 20 percent urbanized to 40 percent urbanized between the end of the Diem era and the early 1970s. Most of this shift involved refugees fleeing the countryside for coastal cities, where they crammed into unproductive situations, further overwhelming the government's meager welfare capabilities. The ground war was a continuing agony for the South Vietnamese.

Throughout this drama, successive Saigon governments (and there were a half dozen, compared to one in Hanoi)[12] sought to build or rebuild linkage between capital and countryside. Yet, in keeping with the republic's elitist political structure, the men controlling these governments also sought to maintain their own financial and political power bases. Seldom did linkage to the countryside take precedence over politics in Saigon. Thieu and Ky actually fought a small war against another general, Thi, in 1966 in DaNang. Then Thieu and Ky turned on each other, Thieu eventually mastering the top spot in the oligarchy. Through it all, anywhere from eight to a dozen South Vietnamese generals (and their wives) were the prime manipulators and beneficiaries of the system. Nevertheless, in spite of the oligarchy's resistance, power *was* gradually decentralized, and the system made less inequitable in the late 1960s and early 1970s due to the pressures of war and pressures from U.S. advisors. But a distorted class and caste system characterized South Vietnam right down to the end: ARVN division commanders still had control of their soldiers' salaries, housing, food, and benefits through to April 1975, when a number of these generals, realizing they could escape neither the communists nor their own troops, committed suicide.

Viewing the long and ultimately unsuccessful effort to reform South Vietnam and build a viable political community in the republic in the midst of war, were there times when reform and changes of leadership might have made a difference? Indeed there were. Ngo Dinh Diem won the legitimate admiration of much of the world between 1954 and 1959 when, against seemingly insurmountable odds, he created a viable state apparatus, got control of the armed forces, and tamed the warring political sects. It was a near miracle of political and personal tenacity. If Diem, who was advised by American and British teams led by Edward Lansdale, and by Robert Thompson and Dennis Duncanson, had gone further and decentralized the state apparatus, placing political development and economic viability above social control and police tactics, South Vietnam might have had a very different future even as Hanoi raised the stakes. The fundamental problems were Diem's Catholicism and Confucianism, and his brother's and sister-in-law's paranoia and ruthlessness. This combination of personal and family idiosyncrasies kept the Diem government from building a viable political community in South Vietnam. Instead, the regime constructed strategic hamlets that trampled on the population's needs. By 1963 Diem found that his family had ruined much of his successful beginning. So the first major decision point came between 1958 and 1962: If Diem had been strong enough to have reformed the system he had created, and gotten his brother and sister-in-law out of the country, the republic would have had a much better chance to deal with the strains that were coming.

The second clear political threshold point was 1968–1971. The Thieu government not only survived the 1968 Tet attacks but actually went on the offensive, arming millions of citizens, sweeping into the security vacuums left by the fighting, decentralizing the administrative apparatus, and producing the first serious land reform in the country's history. The problem was that Thieu, who understood the problem, could not move fast enough or effectively enough to root a viable political community that could withstand the next North Vietnamese invasion. Nor could Thieu overhaul the military caste and spoils system even if he wanted to. When the North Vietnamese army slammed into the republic in March and April 1972, political linkage, tenuous but building, ruptured once again. Three years later the government and army of South Vietnam disintegrated.

Thus, the first irreducible political requirement of victory in Vietnam was a viable, legitimate government in Saigon, which, in the midst of the war, could have built a mature political community linking Saigon to the villages and cities. This never happened.

STRATEGY AND POLICY: THE COSTS OF FIGHTING A DEFENSIVE WAR

A South Vietnamese–American ground invasion of North Vietnam was discussed in Saigon and Washington, and proposals were made by various authorities, most prominently General Cao Van Vien and presidential advisor Walt W. Rostow. By early 1965 South Vietnamese and American authorities favored making North Vietnam pay for the violence it was supporting in South Vietnam; the question was how. It is doubtful the ARVN could have undertaken a successful invasion of North Vietnam given the political chaos in its leadership ranks, and the fact that its units almost never operated in larger than battalion size. And, of course, elected officials in the United States were convinced that a U.S.-sponsored ARVN invasion of North Vietnam would trigger China's and the Soviet's defense pacts with Hanoi, possibly bringing in both Chinese and Russian forces.[13] No one wanted another Korean War. So the less objectionable (and less politically sensitive) *tactic*—and it was a tactic not a strategy—of graduated reprisal bombing against North Vietnam, and against communist forces in Laos and Cambodia, was chosen. Custody was divided among the Air Force and the Navy and Marines, and it was supported in public by all the senior uniformed military and civilian decision-makers implementing the war. The first public doubt about the air campaign's effectiveness surfaced in 1967 when Secretary McNamara began airing his concerns. We also know from detailed studies of North Vietnam's response to the bombing that the DRV not only adjusted to the *Rolling Thunder* bombing campaign, but that it actually helped to mobilize the people, involving them in the country's defense. North Vietnam's control apparatus actually strengthened as a result of the bombing.[14] To my knowledge, no senior United States military commander ever resigned or publicly expressed concern over the bombing campaigns while on active duty. Only afterwards, after the war was lost, did several senior U.S. officers criticize, some bitterly, the operations they helped design and command.[15]

With a ground invasion of North Vietnam ruled out for political reasons by Washington, and not within the capabilities or willpower of the South Vietnamese army, Saigon and Washington chose to fight a strategically defensive war, consigning the strategic offensive to Hanoi. Thus, allied goals were limited, defensive, and designed to preserve South Vietnam, not liberate North Vietnam. By contrast, North Vietnam sought to destroy South Vietnam's government and armed forces, turning the society upside down and communizing it from the bottom up. Even when the communists fell back on the defensive after the Tet 1968 attacks and, again, after the 1972 offensive, these were tactical retreats. Hanoi still held the strategic initiative.

As U.S. material, advisors, and then combat troops began to come in, finding a compatible working relationship between the South Vietnamese and the Americans proved difficult. The U.S. Ambassador, General Maxwell Taylor, spoke to General Thieu and others right after they overthrew the (carefully U.S. nurtured) government of Prime Minister Phat in December 1964:

I told you all clearly at General Westmoreland's dinner that we Americans were tired of coups. . . . I made it clear that all the military plans which I know you would like to carry out are dependent on governmental stability. Now you have made a real mess. We cannot carry you forever if you do things like this . . . I have real problems on the U.S. side. I don't know whether we will continue to support you after this. Why don't you tell your friends before you act?[16]

And, again, in early 1965, Taylor told reporters: "The fighting is going on in four fronts. The government versus the generals, the Buddhists versus the government, the generals versus the ambassador and, I hope, the generals versus the Viet Cong."[17] In short, coalition warfare is the most inefficient, contentious kind of warfare. A search for leverage constantly pervaded the South Vietnamese-American alliance.

Without a combined command, where South Vietnamese units would have come under American commanders (like South Korean units during the Korean War), the United States and South Vietnam began to share the combat effort in the spring and summer of 1965. Designed by General William Westmoreland and his operations deputy, Lieutenant General William DePuy, U.S. ground operations were multibattalion reconnaissance in force—large unit operations like those the United States had employed in Korea and in Europe. Designed to seize the initiative, and relying on superior mobility and firepower, U.S. units took the battle to the enemy *inside South Vietnam*. President Johnson left it to the discretion of General Westmoreland and his commanders how and where to deploy American combat units in the country, and how to use their firepower. No U.S. Ambassador, or South Vietnamese official, fundamentally interfered with this enormous delegation of authority to MACV. As General Westmoreland wrote:

I recognized the necessity to guard against unintended adverse effects stemming from the presence of U.S. combat forces, but I regarded it essential to U.S.-Vietnamese success that U.S. units be available to reinforce and stiffen South Vietnamese forces in the critical areas of high population density. Consequently I planned to build up U.S. forces in and around Saigon and in the populous coastal areas and not to restrict U.S. troops in the Central Highlands.[18]

This was the most fundamental decision made regarding American conduct in Vietnam. And it was a decision with extraordinary political consequences. Millions of South Vietnamese were affected by this decision. By implementing a massive firepower attrition strategy inside a country of contested villages, American strategy did, indeed, produce favorable kill-ratios against communist forces when they chose to fight. But attrition also contributed to hundreds of thousands of South Vietnamese civilian casualties, and the uprooting of millions of people—the creation of a refugee proletariat whose misery the communists skillfully exploited.

Moreover, military attrition in South Vietnam never got Hanoi down to the bottom of its barrel. Because of the sanctuaries, North Vietnam, not the U.S. or the GVN, controlled the tempo of communist force expenditures in South Vietnam. Conducting a war without fronts,[19] COSVN (with some help from U.S. pressure) decentralized NVA/VC attacks into small unit operations. When NVA infiltration was added to Viet Cong recruitment in South Vietnam, and the use of sanctuaries, COSVN was able to maintain a "steady state" of military pressure inside, and adjacent to, South Vietnam. The manpower pool available to the communists made an even bleaker picture. In 1968 North Vietnam had a manpower pool of about 1.8 million males between 15 and 34, only 45 percent serving in the armed forces. Add in recruiting in the South, and the total NVA/VC manpower pool was estimated by U.S. government sources to be 2.3 million. Even at Tet 1968 casualty rates, it would have taken *13 years* to exhaust this manpower reserve. In other words, the "cross-over" point between attrition and replenishment was never even approached.[20] While U.S. kill-ratios against NVA/VC forces were 8 to 1 in the U.S.'s favor, it was almost always COSVN's choice *when* to commit forces, *for how long*, and *when to* disengage. Seldom could U.S./ARVN forces dictate the initiation or pace of a military engagement. Hanoi—not Saigon or Washington—controlled the tempo of violence in South Vietnam. This, then, was the fundamental result of the deliberate U.S./GVN policy of fighting on the strategic defensive—a policy never seriously challenged in the United States by either public officials or private citizens. As Colonel Harry Summers related a conversation in Hanoi in April 1975 with one of his North Vietnamese counterparts: "You know you never defeated us on the battlefield." To which the North Vietnamese colonel replied—"That may be so, but it is also irrelevant."[21]

The other serious flaw in the MACV/ARVN attrition strategy was what it did to South Vietnam's population. Of course, NVA/VC units regularly sought to goad American and South Vietnamese forces into overreactions, and communist forces were quite cynical in making civilians take the brunt of allied reactions. John Paul Vann, the most experienced American in Vietnam, commented on this "judo" tactic several months before his death in combat in June 1972:

In the last decade, I have walked through hundreds of hamlets that have been destroyed in the course of a battle, the majority as the result of the heavier friendly fires. The overwhelming majority of hamlets thus destroyed failed to yield sufficient evidence of damage to the enemy to justify the destruction of the hamlet. Indeed, it has not been unusual to have a hamlet destroyed and find absolutely no evidence of damage to the enemy. . . . The destruction of a hamlet by friendly firepower is an event that will always be remembered and practically never forgiven by those people who lost their homes [and loved ones]."[22]

Of course there were rules of engagement for U.S. forces which were regularly reviewed by troop units, pilots, and gunners. And precautions were taken to avoid the destruction of property and noncombatant life. American fighting men died because of risks taken to spare Vietnamese civilians. "And yet," writes Guenter Lewy

these sensible ideas ran head-on against the mind-set of the conventionally trained officer, who, seeing the war in the perspective of his own expertise [and quick in-and-out combat tour] concentrated on "zapping the Cong" with the weapons he had been trained to use.[23]

With a munitions-intensive, lavish firepower strategy that substituted firepower for manpower, joined with the very questionable practice of H&I (harassment and interdiction) fire, U.S. operations became mind-boggling.[24] A billion dollars of ordnance was expended in two weeks at Khe Sanh in the spring of 1968. During the April 1972 offensive, U.S. forces averaged 250,000 rounds of ammunition *per day*. Moshe Dayan, the Israeli general and future defense minister, toured South Vietnam in 1966 and described an action he witnessed in II Corps: "Along a 200-yard-wide strip between jungle and fence, the American support units laid down no less than 21,000 shells—more than the total volume of artillery fire expended by the Israeli Army during the Suez campaign and the War for Independence together."[25]

Associated with attrition was the implicit policy of refugee generation through compulsory relocations, combat operations, and crop destruction, although many U.S. commanders went to great lengths to shield noncombatants from the fighting. (On the communist side, by contrast, vengeance killings and systematic atrocities such as the murder of 3,000 to 5,000 civilians at Hue during the 1968 Tet offensive were deliberate acts of policy). By the end of 1967, close to a million South Vietnamese were in refugee status.[26] Between 1964 and 1969, as many as 3.5 million South Vietnamese, over 20 percent of the country, had been refugees at one time or another, not including nearly a million more temporarily displaced by the 1968 Tet and post-Tet offensives.[27]

The casualty data tell a vivid story. North Vietnam paid a greater price in military dead but fewer civilian dead than South Vietnam, and there was almost no refugee generation in the DRV. Estimated Communist casualties of 2,747,500 represent one out of every seven North Vietnamese and Viet Cong; that would equate to 32 million American casualties, 12 million of them dead—testimony to the superior ability of communist dictatorships to extract sacrifices from people. But, South Vietnam's casualties also were very serious and—*for the type of society experiencing them*—even more traumatic. War-related hospital admissions in South Vietnam between 1965 and 1974 counted over 475,000 people, representing perhaps 80 percent of those actually wounded, which would give a total of about 571,000 war-related wounded. Somewhere near another 248,000 civilians died as a result of military-related wounds.[28] Guenter Lewy estimated the total South Vietnamese civilian war casualties from 1965 to 1974 to be approximately 1.2 million (342,000 lightly wounded; 571,000 hospitalized; 39,000 assassinated by VC/NVA forces; 248,000 killed). This was an enormous number of people, especially when compared to South Vietnamese military deaths over the same period of about 220,000.[29] The South Vietnamese figure of 1,200,000 casualties was one out of every 17 citizens in the republic; that would equate to 13 million American casualties, 5 million of them dead, when ratioed for population bases—not a "limited war" by any measure. Without strong political institutions or a thorough sense of national identity, those casualties proved too much for South Vietnam. What happened in March and April of 1975 was, in effect, the cumulative result of the many years of damage that these statistics describe.

In summary, the allied strategy of attrition failed in South Vietnam for the following reasons:

—It was constrained by political factors that precluded ARVN–U.S. units from taking the ground war out of South Vietnam and into North Vietnam and its sanctuaries.

—The communist armed forces, and their manpower pool, were not destroyed.

—Lavish allied firepower and insufficient discrimination in applying it inside South Vietnam caused enough damage and dislocation to substantially disrupt the political linkage between the Saigon governments and the people.

Here, then, was a strategy that could not hurt the enemy enough but that hurt our ally too much.

Was there an alternative strategy to attrition—one that could have fostered the needed political community in South Vietnam while also seriously hurting the communists? The answer to that is a qualified yes. Such an alternative strategy would have had to combine population protection and territorial security with either a limited ARVN invasion of North Vietnam or early strategic U.S. air strikes (like *Linebacker I* and *II*) against the DRV. Some ARVN and U.S. officials supported such an alternative strategy, especially conventional military operations against North Vietnam. But, as we have seen, a bold, out-of-country option early in the war was not within the leadership capacity of the ARVN, or within the political strength of the Johnson Administration.

Nevertheless, there were hints, suggestions, of alternative strategies during the war. Although large-scale conventional violence dominated the contest during

1966–1969, and again in 1972 and 1975, modest population security programs operated throughout the conflict. The heyday for population security was from 1967 through 1971 under Thieu, although the Diem government had tried a significant program in the early 1960s. Thieu's later efforts—the Revolutionary Development and Accelerated Pacification Campaigns—won their spurs after the 1968 Tet offensive when the GVN exploited the communist's extraordinary losses and moved to fill the vacuum in the countryside. Prior to 1961, there were a series of short-lived population security programs under the Diem regime, but they were little more than trial and error efforts, poorly administered, insensitive, and coercive.[30]

As President Johnson ordered U.S. combat troop intervention in mid–1965, culminating in over 180,000 U.S. troops in Vietnam by late that year, several modest Vietnamese pacification and local security efforts appeared and then quickly collapsed. New Life Hamlets, *Hop Tac* (Victory), *Chien Thang* (Will to Victory), and Rural Construction were their names.[31] Sensitivity about providing security to the people and about the interrelationships between communist main force units in the hills and the political infrastructure inside the villages was rare among GVN and U.S. officials. Army Chief of Staff General Earl Wheeler's oft-quoted statement that "the essence of the problem in Vietnam is military,"[32] reflected the predominant thinking in the American military chain of command, despite clear acknowledgment by both MACV and Secretary of Defense McNamara of the woefully inadequate political performance of the Saigon government.[33]

By 1966–1967, as much to cope with the human dislocation of the big unit war as to resurrect village security efforts, Washington and Saigon sought to focus attention on more continuous local security in the villages, restoration of more effective, responsible local government, and improved living conditions. In early 1966, the Revolutionary Development (RD) program (Vietnamese name: Rural Development) emerged under the leadership of an energetic, uncorruptable ARVN Brigadier General, Nguyen Duc Thang, and an intense ex-Vietminh cadre training chief, Colonel Nguyen Be.[34] However, new waves of refugees fleeing the conventional fighting and renewed instability in ARVN officer ranks soon ground the RD effort to a near halt. Then, in the spring of 1967, with emphasis from Secretary of Defense McNamara and Deputy Ambassador Robert Komer as head of the MACV staff directorate CORDS (Civil Operations and Revolutionary Development Support), U.S. assistance to Vietnamese population security efforts took on a vigorous new priority.[35] The Vietnamese began to follow suit.

The trends of the Revolutionary Development period were put to their greatest test by the 1968 communist Tet offensive. Tet sent a great shock through the Saigon government, and it precipitated the American disengagement. But the Tet spasm also decimated communist combat forces (especially Viet Cong) in the South—45,000 dead in the first month—perhaps 160,000 communist dead by the end of the year.[36] With over a million refugees generated by the fighting,[37] the core question was which side would fill the vacuum in the countryside. President Thieu took direct command of the situation, and the government re-concentrated on cleaning up the cities and protecting the villages. A series of "Accelerated Pacification Campaigns" began. Despite inefficiency, corruption, and the inability of the GVN to eradicate the communist political infrastructure in the localities, a strategic threshold was crossed. By mid–1969 population security, with more emphasis on Vietnamese territorial security, had become the new core of the Thieu government's strategy.[38] These efforts left much to be desired;[39] but they succeeded well enough that, when combined with the expansion of the RVNAF to over 1.1 million men and other developments adverse to Hanoi's war aims—Thieu's and Nixon's uncompromising stance against a coalition government in Saigon, the "Vietnamization" program, and allied military incursions into Cambodia and Laos—Hanoi concluded that it would have to invade South Vietnam again to save the situation. North Vietnam paid dearly for the invasion. But in the South the ARVN also took serious losses. NVA forces occupied significant portions of Tay Ninh, Phuoc Long, and Binh Long provinces. All of Quang Tri province was lost. On the central coast, Binh Dinh province was seriously jeopardized. Major areas of Quang Tin, Quang Nam, and Thua Thien province lost government security. The invasion skewed the whole war back to a killing attrition contest. Once again, population security was orphaned to the big unit war.

While the 1967 to 1972 period saw an end to the long neglect of population security, it was still clearly a secondary effort compared to the resources going into the big unit war and aerial interdiction in the South. At their height in 1968–1971, the pacification and population security efforts probably did not account for more than one-eighth of the resources the allies were spending. Over the period 1961 to 1973, population security, with its attendant political and economic efforts, probably garnered no more than one-tenth of the war's overall expenditures.[40] Thus, the second irreducible political requirement of victory in the Vietnam war was a major population protection and territorial security strategy in the south combined with extremely punitive out-of-country operations against North Vietnam's war fighting capacity. This alternative combined strategy was never tried.

1973–1975: THE LIMITS OF ENDURANCE

President Richard Nixon was able to use American impatience with the Vietnam War by retaliating with extraordinary force to North Vietnam's Spring 1972 offensive. Combining force, diplomacy, and exploitation of Sino-Soviet differences, Nixon, the major American anticommunist, laid an enormous tactical and strategic reprisal onto the DRV while, at the same time, actually improving U.S. relations with North Vietnam's two principal allies—the U.S.S.R. and the People's Republic of China. Hanoi's bitterness with its friends' behavior was scarcely concealed. All said, April–December 1972 was one of the most dramatic periods in twentieth century American foreign policy, and Nixon was reelected in a landslide victory in the wake of *Linebacker I*. The loser, Senator George McGovern, was so bitter that he went to England after the election and evidently even considered living there permanently. In October 1972 Hanoi balked at coming to terms, but Nixon's victory in early November gave him enough political support to force Hanoi into meaningful negotiations. The President's weapon was *Linebacker II*, the massive twelve-day, December strategic bombing of North Vietnam's heartland. Nixon is reported to have told Admiral Thomas Moorer, Chairman of the Joint Chiefs of Staff: "The bastards have never been bombed like they are going to be bombed this time." The bombing worked: Hanoi quickly got flexible, and by the second week of January, 1973, Le Duc Tho and Henry Kissinger had settled the remaining differences to produce a final version of the peace plan originally negotiated four months earlier. The plan was implemented in March 1973 and American prisoners were airlifted out of North Vietnam to a great wave of relief and patriotism in the United States.

Preceding the events of 1972 and 1973 was the "Vietnamization" program whereby ARVN forces were expanded, U.S. forces withdrawn, and a massive transfer occurred of combat, logistics, communications, training and intelligence functions. By the time of the NVA March 1972 invasion, virtually all American-built bases had been turned over to the South Vietnamese. But, wrote General Bruce Palmer, the South Vietnamese "lacked the means to secure and maintain them. In populated areas the result was widespread looting of supplies, dismemberment of buildings and facilities, and rapid deterioration, while in more remote areas the jungle took over."[41] Untested ARVN divisions were thrown together and deployed where the Americans had once operated. Particularly harmful was the withdrawal of U.S. helicopter support to ARVN units since the Vietnamese had no indigenous aviation units of their own.[42] Gradually President Thieu, having to save ammunition and fuel, began the ominous process of shrinking down the ARVN defense perimeter.

The 1973 Vietnam peace accords diverted American attention (although not that of South Vietnam or North Vietnam) from battlefield realities and political realities that were incompatible with peace. First, between 145,000 and 150,000 North Vietnamese regular troops were left inside South Vietnam, their presence not addressed by the peace accords. President Thieu had repeatedly argued this problem with Washington during the negotiations that preceded the cease-fire. Indeed Thieu was so angry about it and other provisions of the peace plan that Nixon had to send General Alexander Haig and Senator John Stennis to Saigon to induce Thieu's acquiescence under pressure. Simultaneously Henry Kissinger put some of Thieu's more extreme demands to Hanoi so as to make Washington's position seem more reasonable. U.S. bargaining with both Saigon and Hanoi became frenetic.[43] Finally, when Thieu balked again, following the December 1972 bombing campaign, Nixon gave his final ultimatum to Saigon: Close ranks now or see an end to U.S. military and economic assistance. "Decide now,"

Nixon told Thieu, "whether you desire to continue our alliance or whether you want me to seek a settlement with the enemy which serves U.S. interests alone." Thieu gave in.[44]

The other major flaw in the peace accords included the stipulation that while the two Vietnams could replace material on a one-for-one basis of like terms *in the South*, these restrictions did not apply to military assistance flowing into North Vietnam.[45] Naturally Hanoi quickly turned the Ho Chi Minh trails into a wide open logistics pipeline. "The Trail," wrote General Palmer, "was converted into a complex of wide macadam roads, concrete bridges, and permanent drainage systems so that Hanoi was able to move major logistics units from Laos into South Vietnam and build up large supply dumps inside South Vietnam."[46]

Then in the Summer of 1973, as NVA infiltration resumed, the American Congress passed the Copper-Church amendment, which forbade using any more American airpower in Southeast Asia. South Vietnam would be on its own in dealing with new North Vietnamese invasions—the American material lifeline now being its sole source of ammunition, spare parts, and fuel. Draconian measures were applied in South Vietnam: Deadlined tanks, aircraft, and armored personnel carriers increased as ammunition, fuel, and spare parts dwindled. Aircraft and vehicles were cannibalized; medical supplies were cut to the bone. As U.S. aid shrank, but North Vietnam's infiltration continued, President Thieu began closing outlying fire bases that stood in the way of the NVA. Gradually, South Vietnam's defense posture shriveled.

1974 began ominously for the Republic of Vietnam, with both sides suffering heavy casualties. NVA units in the south, now receiving ample resupply from a secure homeland feeding the extended all-weather logistical system, also free from attack, began setting up for the kill. By late 1974–early 1975, North Vietnamese combat forces inside South Vietnam were up to 200,000, with an additional 100,000 combat support and logistics troops. Communist armored vehicles, mostly tanks, had risen to 700—twice the ARVNs.[47] By March 1975 it was the beginning of the end. The North Vietnamese offensive began in the II Corps area with diversionary attacks on Kontum and Pleiku. ARVN forces panicked and retreated. Hordes of refugees crammed the escape routes. Then came major offensives against Ban Me Thuot, below the DMZ (Demilitarized Zone), and toward Saigon from the Cambodian bases. The contagion spread to DaNang and from there down the coast. By early April, Hanoi was packing its armor and infantry into the outskirts of Saigon. In three more agonizing weeks a fifteen-year defense effort was finished.

Thus, Hanoi, with Soviet and Chinese support, was able to outlast South Vietnam and the United States. By politically and militarily protracting the war past the allies' endurance, Hanoi traded space and casualties for time— ultimately the determining factor. As a result, the third irreducible political requirement for victory in Vietnam—an allied capacity to outlast Hanoi—fell apart.

CONCLUSION

The Second Indochina War could have had a different outcome. A differently organized and defended South Vietnam could well have survived Hanoi's attacks, and "victory" could have been achieved—a victory defined as a comparatively free, noncommunist South Vietnam, decreasingly dependent on external aid.

First and foremost was the problem of political development and population security in South Vietnam. No sufficiently viable political community emerged in South Vietnam despite years of effort, changes of government, and resources expended. The Diem government was traditional, Catholic, and personalized. It was a family regime—a patriarchy—incapable of organizing South Vietnamese society in a manner that would get enough people to identify with and fight for the national government. The officers who overthrew Diem and formed their own governments—Minh, Khanh, Ky, and Thieu—shifted the focus of power to cliques within the armed forces. Despite Thieu's commendable efforts between 1967 and 1971, in the midst of heavy fighting, to decentralize power and push resources out to the villages, his priorities were constantly contested by the other generals. Thieu's plans were further sidetracked when Hanoi slammed its great wall of military pressure against the Republic in April 1972. Population security was shoved aside once again. Ultimately, Vietnamese leaders in Saigon, like the communists who came to power in Hanoi, had to fashion a system of political authority that linked the national government and the villages into a mutually supportive, legitimate and sustainable national community. Ho Chi Minh did this in North Vietnam by liquidating his opposition, amputating and co-opting their organizations, reorganizing, and penetrating all of North Vietnamese society with the Lao Dong Workers Party. When Ho and the party turned their full attention to subverting South Vietnam in 1959, he had been organizing and preparing the ground for revolution for 30 years. His accomplishment was extraordinarily repulsive in what it did to the millions of human beings who resisted, but as an exercise in the conquest of power it was a masterpiece of social engineering. This, in essence, but with obviously different values and treatment of human life, is what the Saigon governments needed to do. They needed to develop South Vietnam politically, build power, and imbed it within the population so as to involve the people in their own defense and welfare. Not an easy task, nor can it be done quickly. It took Diem five years simply to stabilize his control of the levers of power in South Vietnam's population centers. By then, 1959, Hanoi had put in motion its plan to destroy the Republic.

Secondly, both the political costs of the US/GVN attrition strategy and the political constraints upon it proved too high. While attrition did major damage to the main force units, COSVN *chose* to commit, attrition never drove NVA/VC units down to unacceptable levels. Moreover, the scope and intensity of allied firepower, when exploited by Hanoi's hostaging of South Vietnamese populated areas, resulted in very serious damage to the Republic. The political costs of the uprooting and damage to hundreds of thousands of people were intolerably high. Too many RVN citizens concluded that neither Saigon nor its U.S. ally cared sufficiently about their welfare. Strategically, Hanoi was largely able to control the level of violence inside South Vietnam (and, therefore, the attrition of its own forces), by committing or withdrawing them from combat at times and places of its choosing. Thus, on balance, North Vietnam essentially dictated the strategic tempo of the ground war, while the allies dominated the tactical outcomes (the "battles"). Few more telling lessons about the value of sanctuaries and the paralyzing effect of political constraints can be demonstrated than the fact that Hanoi hid its forces just across South Vietnam's borders, while Washington and Saigon declined, until very late in the war, to attack those sanctuaries. Would an ARVN invasion have triggered Chinese or Soviet intervention? From the hindsight of the U.S. strategic bombing of North Vietnam in 1972, and Hanoi's reluctance to allow a major foreign presence inside the DRV, it appears that a limited ARVN invasion of North Vietnam would not have precipitated Chinese or Soviet intervention as occurred in the Korean War. If Saigon and Washington had clearly signaled that an ARVN move was not designed to liberate North Vietnam, but simply to raise the price to the DRV for its own invasion of the RVN, it is likely that the war would have stayed limited.

Third, by early 1973 it was clear that the United States was finished with Indochina, and it was just a question of time until the entire U.S. combat presence left. In the summer of 1973, the Congress passed the Cooper-Church amendment, which prohibited any further U.S. armed intervention in Indochina. Hanoi undoubtedly understood what this meant even if the Thieu government in Saigon, still clinging to the hope that the Americans would come back when Hanoi reattacked, did not. The Thieu government, wedded to the U.S. style munitions-intensive defense system, had no choice but to shrink its defense perimeter to the bone as U.S. aid dwindled month by month.

Ultimately, of course, despite the massive external assistance to both Vietnams, it came down to a contest between the Vietnamese, as it had so many times before in their many centuries of conflict and violence against both themselves and foreign invaders. And, as is the case in revolutions, the heart of the problem lay in *politics*, not in force. How could you, as one close observer asked, solve the challenge of "reforming and redistributing power in a political system under severe internal strain?"[48] The South Vietnamese, despite their extraordinary effort to stave off Hanoi, never solved that basic political problem. Robert Shaplen's insight on the situation five years before the end unfortunately became the most accurate epitaph on the story: "And so it goes—a kind of compulsive mutual-vivisection society, in which everyone wants to cut everyone else up to determine the cause of the national disease, which may be incurable."[49] That South Vietnam and the United States ultimately failed, and in the process clearly contributed to their failure by the ways in which they fought, requires no further elaboration. But, as Lewy writes, "The fact that South Vietnam, abandoned by its ally, finally succumbed to a powerful and ruthless antagonist does not prove that this policy could not have had a less tragic ending."[50] The sad fate of the people of Indochina since 1975—the millions who have had to endure the communist regimes in Hanoi, Phnom Penh, and Vientiane, or in desperation have taken their chances on the open seas and in the refugee camps— gives vivid testimony to what people will do for freedom, imperfect though it is, in flight from what they can no longer endure.

NOTES

1. Michael Howard, "The Use and Abuse of Military History," *Parameters*, 11:1 (March 1981), p. 14.
2. This discussion draws, in part, on Lawrence E. Grinter, "How They Lost: Doctrines, Strategies, and Outcomes of the Vietnamese War," *Asian Survey* (December 1975), pp. 1119–1121.
3. This is Jeffrey Race's basic thesis. See especially Chapter IV of his *War Comes to Long An: Revolutionary Conflict in a Vietnamese Province* (Berkeley: University of California Press, 1972).
4. See Ithiel de Sola Pool, "Political Alternatives to the Viet Cong," *Asian Survey* 7:8 (August, 1967), pp. 555–556.
5. Samuel Huntington, *Political Order in Changing Societies* (New Haven, Conn.: Yale University Press, 1966), pp. 335, 343.
6. Not that Diem could not also be rough. His outmaneuvering of the Binh Xuyen gangsters, the Cao Dai and Hoa Hao sects, and a variety of armed French agents utilized cunning, money, and force. In these actions Diem had CIA assistance. William S. Turley, *The Second Indochina War: A Short Political and Military History, 1954–1975* (Boulder, Colo.: Westview Press, 1986), pp. 12–14.
7. Douglas Pike, *Viet Cong* (Cambridge: MIT Press, 1966), pp. 9–10.
8. Lucien Pye, "The Roots of Insurgency and the Commencement of Rebellions," in Harry Eckstein, *Internal War: Problems and Approaches* (New York: The Free Press, 1964), p. 161.
9. Lawrence E. Grinter, "South Vietnam: Pacification Denied," *South-East Asian SPECTRUM*, 3:4 (July 1975), pp. 62–64.
10. Robert Shaplen, "Letter from Vietnam," *The New Yorker* (24 June 1972), p. 70.
11. See, for example the appraisal by Craig R. Whitney, "Pacification Hopes Battered in Vietnam, *The New York Times* (21 June 1972), pp. 1, 14.
12. The inherent instability in South Vietnamese political life, across both military and civilian strata, was aptly demonstrated between 1963 and 1968. The successor regime to Diem, the Tho government, lasted 86 days; General Khanh's government lasted 260 days; Mr. Huong's government lasted 64 days; Mr. Oanh's government lasted 19 days; the civilian Quat government lasted 112 days; the Air Vice Marshall Ky government had five major reshufflings. In 1967 Ky was replaced at the top by Thieu who, while lasting until 1975, undertook numerous cabinet reshufflings. See I. Milton Sacks, "Restructuring Government in South Vietnam," *Asian Survey* (August 1967), pp. 518–520.
13. The weighing of risks versus benefits leading up to the initial U.S. bombing campaign of 1965, and the views of President Johnson and his principal advisors, are analyzed in Colonel Dennis M. Drew, *Rolling Thunder 1965: Anatomy of a Failure*, ARI Report No. AU-ARI-CP–86–3 (Maxwell AFB, Ala.: Air University Press, 1986), pp. 28–42.

14. See Jon M. Van Dyke, *North Vietnam's Strategy for Survival* (Palo Alto: Pacific Books, 1972), especially pp. 78–110.

15. See, for example, Admiral Ulysses S. Grant Sharp, U.S. Navy, (Ret.), *Strategy for Defeat* (San Rafael, Ca: Presidio Press, 1978).

16. Taylor's remarks are excerpted from an Embassy Saigon airgram to the State Department on 24 December 1964 as reprinted in *The New York Times* (14 June 1971), pp. 29–30, as cited in Lawrence E. Grinter, "Bargaining Between Saigon and Washington: Dilemmas of Linkage Politics During War" in *Orbis* (Fall 1974), p. 858.

17. Taylor is quoted in Richard Crithfield, *The Long Charade: Political Subversion in the Vietnam War* (New York: Harcourt, Brace and World, 1966), p. 96.

18. General William C. Westmoreland, USA, and Admiral Ulysses S. Grant Sharp, USN, *Report on the War in Vietnam as of 30 June 1968* (Washington: USGPO, 1969) p. 99. Also see pp. 114, 132.

19. See Thomas C. Thayer, "How to Analyze a War Without Fronts, Vietnam 1965–72," *Journal of Defense Research*, Series B Tactical Warfare, 7B:3 (Fall 1975).

20. Guenter Lewy, *America in Vietnam* (New York: Oxford University Press, 1978), pp. 83–84.

21. Harry G. Summers, Jr. *On Strategy: The Vietnam War in Context* (Carlisle Barracks, Penn.: U.S. Army War College, April 1981), p. 1.

22. Vann's memo cited in Guenter Lewy, "Some Political-Military Lessons of the Vietnam War" *Parameters* 14:1 (Spring 1984), p. 8.

23. Lewy, *America in Vietnam*, p. 96.

24. The U.S. Army's near obsession with firepower in Vietnam and some of its results are detailed in Andrew F. Krepinevich, Jr., *The Army and Vietnam* (Baltimore: The Johns Hopkins University Press, 1986), pp. 170, 190–91, 196–205, 222, 224.

25. Arthur Schlesinger, Jr., *Bitter Heritage: Vietnam and American Democracy, 1941–1966* (Boston: Houghton Mifflin, 1968), p. 60.

26. Lewy, *America in Vietnam*, p. 65.

27. Ibid., p. 108.

28. Ibid., p. 244.

29. Ibid., p. 451.

30. Grinter, "Pacification Denied," pp. 49–55.

31. Ibid., pp. 56–59.

32. Quoted in Roger Hilsman, *To Make a Nation: The Politics of Foreign Policy in the Administration of John F. Kennedy* (Garden City, NY: Doubleday, 1967), p. 426.

33. See *The Pentagon Papers*, IV. C.1, pp. 30–34, 40.

34. Douglas S. Blaufarb, *The Counterinsurgency Era: U.S. Doctrine and Performance, 1950 to the Present* (New York: Free Press, 1977), pp. 225–27.

35. See Robert W. Komer, *Bureaucracy at War: U.S. Performance in the Vietnam Conflict* (Boulder, Colo.: Westview Press, 1986), pp. 115–131.

36. Richard A. Hunt, "The Challenge of Counterinsurgency," in John Schlight, editor, *Second Indochina War Symposium: Papers and Commentary* (Washington: Center of Military History, United States Army, 1986), p. 136.

37. Sharp and Westmoreland, *Report on the War in Vietnam*, p. 170; and Robert Shaplen, *The Road from War: Vietnam 1965–1970* (New York: Harper and Row, 1970), p. 191.

38. Robert W. Komer, "Clear, Hold and Rebuild," *Army* (May 1970), p. 21; "Pacification: A Look Back and Ahead," *Army* (June 1970), p. 24; and MACV/CORDS,

"Four Year Community Defense and Local Development," Saigon: MACV, 10 January 1973; Blaufarb, *The Counterinsurgency Era*, pp. 263–68; and Tran Dinh Tho, *Pacification*, Indochina Monograph, (Washington, DC: U.S. Army Center of Military History, 1980), pp. 150–55, 167, 169. Also of relevance is John Paul Vann, opening statement, February 18, 1970, before U.S. Congress, Senate Committee on Foreign Relations, *Vietnam: Policy and Prospects*, 1970, Hearings, p. 90; Allan E. Goodman, "South Vietnam and the New Security," *Asian Survey* (February 1972), p. 126; and Roy L. Prosterman, "Land Reform as Foreign Aid," *Foreign Policy* (Spring 1972), p. 135.

39. And in spite of the expansion of South Vietnamese territorial forces (Rural Forces [RF] and Provincial Forces [PF]) in numbers, their equipment and funding was extremely poor. Their very good overall combat record is all the more remarkable when one realizes how orphaned they were by U.S. and GVN conventional military operations: while accounting for 12–30 percent of all NVA/VC combat deaths (depending on the year), the RF and PF consumed only 2–4 percent of the total cost of the war. Krepinevich, *The Army and Vietnam*, p. 22.

40. Washington's operational priorities in the war were revealed in the allocation of funds. In fiscal year 1969, for example, American ground, air, and naval actions in the Vietnam theater took 82 percent of total costs. Expenditures for civil programs, including pacification, amounted to *only 4 percent* that year! The air war alone cost 47 percent of total U.S. expenditures. Even in 1971, a year of much reduced fighting, two-thirds of U.S. outlays went to the main force war, while Vietnamese territorial forces and the police received a mere *2.5 percent* of U.S. funds that year. Hunt, "The Challenge of Counterinsurgency," in Schlight *Second Indochina War Symposium*, pp. 123–124.

41. General Bruce Palmer, *The 25-Year War: America's Military Role in Vietnam* (New York: Simon and Schuster, 1984), p. 118.

42. Ibid., p. 119.

43. See Grinter, "Bargaining between Saigon and Washington," *ORBIS* (Fall 1974), pp. 863–64.

44. Excerpts of Nixon's messages to Thieu are in Henry A. Kissinger, *White House Years* (Boston: Little, Brown, 1979), pp. 1459–60, 1462, 1469.

45. Palmer, *The 25-Year War: America's Military Role in Vietnam*, p. 130.

46. Ibid., p. 132.

47. Ibid., p. 142.

48. Blaufarb, *The Counterinsurgency Era*, p. 277.

49. Robert Shaplen, "Letter from Saigon," *New Yorker* (31 January 1970), p. 55.

50. Lewy, *America in Vietnam*, p. 441.

4

Alan L. Gropman

Lost Opportunities: The Air War in Vietnam, 1961–1973

The Vietnam war was a humiliating, exceptionally expensive, and probably unnecessary American defeat. Had air power been used to its fullest conventional potential, America would not have spilled its blood and squandered its treasure uselessly.

A short essay on the air strategy of the Vietnam war defies generalization. The conflict went on endlessly, numerous decisionmakers had roles, and the views of these players changed. Some policy and strategy formulaters (mostly civilians joined initially by a few military) saw the war as essentially a counterinsurgency and considered the defeat of the Viet Cong in South Vietnam their major objective. Others viewed the war as an effort by North Vietnam to conquer South Vietnam. As it turned out the latter view was accurate: today indigenous South Vietnamese communists are nowhere near the center of power in Ho Chi Minh City.

But the point of this essay is not to upbraid those who saw the war incorrectly for that particular error. The mistake that mattered was not that one, but the failure to realize that even if the war had been an insurgency, victory could be achieved only by shutting off outside assistance to the guerrillas at or very near its source in North Vietnam. There have been no successful counterinsurgencies without effective interdiction of outside assistance.[1] As it happened, Hanoi was the direct aggressor; the war could be decided only in North Vietnam. Striking the heart of North Vietnam and its major logistic arteries was the key to victory, regardless of one's views of the nature of the conflict. Unfortunately, attacking the capillaries in southern North Vietnam, South Vietnam, and Laos was the chosen policy. It squandered assets and led to defeat.

Some in the Johnson administration feared Chinese (or Soviet) involvement in the war should bombing of North Vietnam become intolerable to them. The rationale for such apprehensions was (and remains) unclear. Certainly, fears of Secretary of Defense Robert S. McNamara and his key advisor on air strategy,

John McNaughton, should have been dissipated by Chinese and Soviet quiescence during times of relatively intense United States bombing activity. In any case, whatever excuse Lyndon B. Johnson and his advisors had did not apply to President Richard M. Nixon and his advisors, given the moves by the Chinese in 1970 to open relations with the United States and simultaneous Soviet attempts to enhance détente.

It appears that Lyndon Johnson—the president most responsible for the debacle—took advice on the war from people who understood the liabilities of air power but not its benefits. These people took counsel of their fears and promulgated a strategyless policy that produced disaster. They formulated an impotent application of air power that aimed only at protracting the war until Hanoi and the Viet Cong could stand it no longer. In the end, the American people's tolerance for pain proved to be shorter lived than the North Vietnamese leadership's persistence in accepting destruction of superficial national assets in pursuit of their lifelong dream.

The majority of the Joint Chiefs in 1964 argued that North Vietnam was the enemy and air power was a key to success in the war.[2] The Chiefs and the Pacific Command developed a strategy that aimed at sealing off North Vietnam from outside logistics support by mining harbors and attacking shipping, and further hampering Communist operations in South Vietnam by severing lines of communication to the south.[3] All proponents of this strategy recognized the need to prevent Chinese and Soviet supplies from reaching guerrillas and North Vietnamese regulars in South Vietnam. But Air Force leaders also knew something more: attacking capillary-sized lines of communication far from Hanoi (the industrial, transportation, and administrative center of North Vietnam) would be ineffective because these capillaries could be multiplied almost indefinitely by the enemy. Ports, railroad marshalling yards, and major rail and highway chokepoints close to Hanoi presented the critical targets of choice.[4]

Consequently, the Air Force Chief of Staff, General Curtis E. LeMay, argued forcefully for an immediate and concentrated attack against strategic targets in the Hanoi-Haiphong area. He knew interdiction elsewhere was not likely to be decisive. He was opposed by Generals Earl G. Wheeler, Army Chief of Staff, and Maxwell Taylor, Chairman of the Joint Chiefs of Staff, also an Army officer, who preferred a more gradual increase in air pressure on North Vietnam; they believed the war had to be won in South Vietnam and that the Army should carry that burden. Wheeler also believed an air campaign should support the war in South Vietnam chiefly through close air support.

The Army view in 1964 was essentially in line with Secretary of Defense Robert S. McNamara's own views. He called for two main air missions (in addition to essential airlift): close air support by the Air Force of Army units and interdiction of enemy lines of communication in and near South Vietnam. The Secretary believed, without any evidence—and he persisted in this belief until he left office—that the implicit *threat* of air attacks on military industrial targets would influence the North Vietnamese to restrain their support of the

Viet Cong. If an attack were to be made against North Vietnam, it should be only to *demonstrate* resolve to expand the conflict. While he permitted striking targets just north of the demilitarized zone separating North from South Vietnam, he reserved targets deeper in the north for strike only if the Hanoi government failed to respond to United States' pressure.[5]

The Joint Chiefs of Staff, however, looking to the future, developed a list of strategic targets in North Vietnam. Initially there were 94 targets considered to have a direct relationship to North Vietnam's war-making capacity and the will to fight (by 1967 this list had grown to 244 targets).[6]

Pierce Arrow, the aerial response to the 1964 North Vietnamese attacks in the Gulf of Tonkin, was the first of a series of "tit for tat" bombing reprisals. Targets were released for attack a few at a time in reaction to North Vietnamese activities, rather than on the basis of a comprehensive American air strategy.

Significantly, these strikes were oriented toward achieving some particular effect upon the ground war in South Vietnam and not on affecting the will or capability of the North Vietnamese to fight. McNamara, supported by his civilian and ranking Army advisors, had argued that bombing a few targets in North Vietnam would demonstrate the potential costs to Hanoi and therefore restrain the communist government. But Ho Chi Minh's response to the *Pierce Arrow* attacks was not restrained. He moved 30 jet fighters from China to Hanoi's main military airfield. The air attacks did not shock Ho; they simply spurred him to start working on what was to become a superb air defense system of jet fighters, surface-to-air missiles, and anti-aircraft artillery.[7]

Further demonstrating that limited retaliatory attacks were not reducing their will to fight, the Viet Cong and North Vietnamese also stepped up attacks against American airfields. These attacks led the Joint Chiefs in November 1964 to propose a series of strikes against North Vietnam based on their list of 94 targets. President Johnson rejected this proposal, but it served to put *all* of the Joint Chiefs on record in favor of more aggressive air strikes against North Vietnam. Despite the consensus among the generals and admirals, McNamara advised Johnson to continue his gradualistic approach. President Johnson, faced with serious domestic priorities following President Kennedy's assassination and the rising civil rights revolution in the United States, retained total control of air strikes in Indochina from the first strikes in 1964 until he left office in January 1969. Targets were, in the view of Gelb and Betts, doled out "abstentiously and with detailed personal attention in the Tuesday luncheons to which no military officer was regularly invited until late in 1967." Johnson and McNamara, in General Momyer's view, "regulated the pace of escalation personally by minimizing autonomy in the field and discouraging the development of comprehensive campaign plans."[8]

The President and his Secretary of Defense were stymied by their fears and their inadequate understanding of the nature of war. Besides worrying that dramatic strikes might prompt Soviet or Chinese intervention (although there had been no serious response to American attacks to date), Johnson feared that such bombing might impede chances for negotiations (although Hanoi had shown no willingness to compromise) and that bombing, in any case, was not cost effective[9] (as if defeat had no price tag). The debate went on until the end of the war; it was about whether bombing was a political signal or a military means to political ends.[10]

To raise South Vietnamese morale and to increase the pressure incrementally after a series of attacks by the Viet Cong and North Vietnamese on Pleiku and Qui Nhon, a campaign called *Flaming Dart* was begun in February 1965. The next month it evolved into a more systematic air campaign called *Rolling Thunder*. The latter involved strikes on lines of communication in North Vietnam below the 19th parallel (well south of Hanoi and Haiphong) and elsewhere.

General LeMay retired in January 1965, still calling for a truly strategic air campaign; his successor, General John C. McConnell, was no less vocal. McConnell argued the United States needed to concentrate on destroying *the center* of the North's logistics network, not its tributary aspects. Despite McConnell's view, the Secretary of Defense continued to maintain that the primary role of air power was to support ground forces in South Vietnam.[11]

In early 1965, the Joint Chiefs advocated a four-phase strategic attack against North Vietnam. All agreed with McNamara on the need to continue an appropriate level of close air support of the South Vietnamese and American troops in South Vietnam but, without strategic attack on North Vietnam, the Chiefs knew that the United States was in for a prolonged war of attrition. The Chiefs believed a strategic air attack that destroyed the ports, mined the harbors, completely interrupted the transportation net, and destroyed ammunition and supply areas in the heartland of Vietnam would convince Hanoi that South Vietnam was not worth the ultimate price—destruction of their society.[12] The Chiefs' proposal was not approved.

Meanwhile, Hanoi responded to piecemeal air attacks on southern North Vietnam by building comprehensive air defenses. American reconnaissance, as early as April 1965, had revealed the construction of Soviet surface-to-air missile sites in North Vietnam. The military had immediately asked for permission to strike the sites before they were completed. The Department of Defense refused that permission. General Westmoreland quoted Assistant Secretary of Defense John McNaughton on Hanoi's air defense missiles: "Putting them in is just a political ploy by the Russians to appease Hanoi." (To McNaughton and McNamara, it seemed largely a matter of signals.) "We won't bomb the sites and that will be a signal to North Vietnam not to use them."[13] The illogic cost the United States hundreds of lives, billions of dollars in destroyed aircraft, and the imprisonment of hundreds of American Air Force and Navy aircrew members. In response to the July 1965 fighter shootdown, the President and Secretary of Defense authorized strikes against only those surface-to-air missile sites that were actually firing at United States aircraft. Even this authority did not extend to targets above the 20th parallel.[14] Over the course of the war, while the surface-to-air missiles accounted for about 20 percent of the United States air losses, they forced changes in tactics that made American aircraft vulnerable to other ordnance.

Johnson's key civilian advisors did not understand how air power had contributed to victory in World War II, especially in the Pacific theater, nor how it had helped end the ugly stalemate in Korea in 1953 with the threatened Manchurian bombing. The advisors also would not listen to those who did. Their misreading of the enemy, combined with their misunderstanding of air power, led to a series of bombing halts (coordinated with bad weather) in the hope that the North Vietnamese, with relief from limited pressure, would see the error of their ways and negotiate a peace or withdraw from South Vietnam. McNaughton, McNamara, and Johnson devised an air strategy of, in the view of Leslie Gelb and Richard Betts, "uncoordinated carrots and sticks" that, by smashing nothing of great value, succeeded in signaling nothing. Between 1965 and 1968, President Johnson halted the bombing 16 times and publicly promulgated 71 peace initiatives—the last coming upon his dramatic March 1968 withdrawal from the presidential campaign of 1968.[15] Hanoi was not impressed, except perhaps with its own ability to drive the American political process.

In early 1966, Assistant Secretary McNaughton wrote a memo that characterized the Defense Department view of bombing North Vietnam. Bombings, he asserted, were to interdict infiltration, bring about negotiations, provide a bargaining counter—we will stop bombing if you stop fighting—in negotiations (which he called "minuets"), and sustain South Vietnamese and United States morale. He doubted that, short of drastic action against the North Vietnamese population, an air campaign could persuade Hanoi to come to the table.

McNaughton recognized that the Air Force, with conventional munitions, was capable of destroying industrial targets, locks and dams on the waterways, and significant portions of the population. The first (industry and infrastructure) he rejected because of North Vietnam's primarily rural economy; the last (population) because it might produce a "counterproductive wave of revulsion abroad and at home." Paradoxically, he thought that flooding might have some merit. But he ended up arguing against strategic bombing and supported strikes "only as frequently as is required to keep alive Hanoi's fear of the future." McNaughton looked on air power as a sophisticated "ratchet" to tighten or loosen the pressure on Hanoi to alter the politburo's mood.[16]

McNamara argued before the Congress in 1965 that U.S. objectives were "limited only to destruction of the insurgencies and aggression directed by North Vietnam against the political institutions of South Vietnam." He wanted to convince Ho Chi Minh by close air support and interdiction in southern North Vietnam, South Vietnam, and elsewhere, that North Vietnam could not conquer South Vietnam.[17] Here McNamara was proposing a policy of attrition and protracted war. In such a war, however, Hanoi merely needed to outlast the United States, a casualty-sensitive country fighting a war half the world away, with its major national interests elsewhere. The Joint Chiefs disagreed with McNamara's view of the conflict, arguing the war was no longer an insurgency but a conventional conflict that demanded an air campaign not confined to South Vietnam. In any event, even if the war were an insurgency, no victory could be achieved so long as Hanoi could run in supplies and equipment to their forces in the South without grave risk to their own centers.[18] *The task which Johnson and McNamara gave air power—to sever the supply system by striking only its terminal phases—was both exceptionally costly and fundamentally unfeasible.*

In late 1966, having rejected a strategic air campaign, McNamara counseled the President that there was no way to end the war soon and that the country needed to "gird" itself "openly for a longer war."[19] But he lost his nerve less than two years later and asked to be relieved from office. It seemed that few senior civilians in the Department of Defense in 1965 and 1966, when they were counseling gradualism, recognized the frustrations building in the American population, although a similar reaction had happened before within all of their memories. During the Korean war, President Harry Truman had been driven out of the presidential campaign of 1952 (as Johnson was in 1968) because he could not bring the war to a rapid conclusion.

The preceding brief analysis shows that the policy governing the application of air power in Vietnam was badly flawed. With this fact in mind, let us now review air operations between 1961 and 1972, paying particular attention to the significant air efforts in the two climactic years—1968 and 1972.

AIR POWER AT WAR

In late 1961 President Kennedy sent a combat unit of air commandos equipped with T–28s, B–26s, and other "vintage" aircraft to South Vietnam. Thereafter, United States combat air power in Vietnam slowly grew, but by the end of the year there were still only 117 American aircraft there, 50 of which were strike capable. By the end of 1965, however, there were about 500 American aircraft based in Vietnam as well as United States Navy aircraft carriers off the Vietnamese coast. Tactical air warfare in Vietnam was by then being fought on a large scale. The initial hope of the Defense Department had been that the Air Force would be used only to train the South Vietnamese Air Force, but the strength of the North Vietnamese and Viet Cong compelled the United States to up the ante dramatically to prevent a South Vietnamese defeat.[20]

South Vietnam was in desperate straits in 1965, with one military coup following another and the United States anxiously trying to find ways to bolster South Vietnamese defenses and morale. To improve South Vietnamese spirits, Washington openly talked about deploying additional American forces to Vietnam and the White House lifted restrictions on the use of United States aircraft over South Vietnam. As an exclamation point, in June 1965, B–52s dropped their first bombs on targets in South Vietnam.[21]

During 1966 American troop strength continued to grow, reaching a total of

325,000 troops, and several American allies—Korea, Australia, and New Zealand—also supplied forces. The growth of American forces apparently induced an increase in North Vietnamese forces, which in turn caused another expansion in American forces. By the beginning of 1968 there were about 500,000 Americans in South Vietnam. Approximately 10 percent were United States Air Force personnel.[22]

Events in 1968, especially the Tet offensive, changed the political and social climate in the United States to the point that President Johnson dropped from the presidential campaign. It is useful here to dwell momentarily on the contributions of air power to two important military campaigns of 1968—the Tet offensive and the siege of Khe Sanh.

During the Tet offensive, air power played a key, although certainly not the major, role in keeping Hanoi from accomplishing its military objectives. Beginning on January 31, violating a holiday truce, the Viet Cong and North Vietnamese Army launched simultaneous attacks on 36 of the 44 provisional capitals, five of the six autonomous cities, 23 airfields, and numerous district capitals and hamlets. Apparently General Giap hoped the South Vietnamese army would disintegrate and the people of South Vietnam would rally to the Communist cause. Fortunately, because of intelligence warning, the American Seventh Air Force had entered the Tet "Truce" on full alert,[23] and was able to support South Vietnamese and American ground forces as they overcame their initial shock and bravely fought back.

Within hours the enemy had seized temporary control of ten provisional capitals and succeeded in penetrating such important cities as Quang Tri, DaNang, Hue, Nha Trang, Kontum, and even Saigon, including the grounds of the American Embassy compound in the center of the city. But except in Hue, the enemy was largely cleaned out after the first several days of the offensive. Despite the heavy simultaneous demands placed upon 7th Air Force to help defend Khe Sanh, 7th Air Force, Marine and Navy strike aviation and Air Force airlift were critical factors in the enemy's tactical defeats on the battlefield.

Air power did everything expected of it. Between January 30 and February 25, more than 16,000 strike sorties were flown by the Air Force, with additional thousands flown by the Marines and Navy, all in support of American and Vietnamese ground forces. And airlift—some 280 aircraft—moved troops rapidly wherever needed to thwart an enemy attack. Because of American airlift, the enemy's disruption of surface lines of communication during the Tet offensive was of little value to him. At one point more than 12,000 troops were moved in hours from the southern Military regions to the most threatened area—Military Region I—to frustrate any plans General Giap might have had to separate part of that region from South Vietnam.[24]

Retaking Hue proved to be the most difficult problem. NVA regulars moved into the inner city and hung on. Communist cadres began systematically executing South Vietnamese civilians. Marine, Navy, and Air Force fighters flew hundreds of sorties to support Marines and the 1st Air Cavalry Division as they battled house-to-house to drive out the enemy. It took almost a month, but by the 25th of February, Hue's inner city was again in friendly hands.[25] North Vietnamese and Viet Cong losses were exceptionally heavy. 5,000 Communist troops were lost at Hue alone. Overall enemy losses during the month-long Tet attack were about 45,000 killed. The Viet Cong was never again a major factor in the war—the overwhelming burden of fighting now falling to regular North Vietnamese troops.

Nonetheless, the Tet offensive proved to be a political disaster for the United States. Although the battles failed to have the desired effect upon the South Vietnamese population, they caused many Americans to doubt the possibility that the United States could ever achieve its goals in Vietnam. Tet broke the back of the Johnson administration's policies in Vietnam and ushered in the start of U.S. withdrawals a year later. The domestic political loss notwithstanding, American airpower had helped to demonstrate to Hanoi that it could not succeed in conquering South Vietnam as long as the United States retained its military forces there.

Similarly, with the North Vietnamese siege of the Marine base at Khe Sanh, whatever their intention—and some think it was to repeat the capture of a large body of defenders as he had done in Dien Bien Phu in 1954—air power this time saw to it that Hanoi failed while also suffering enormous losses. About a week before General Vo Nguyen Giap launched the Tet offensive, he laid siege to the U. S. Marine fire base at Khe Sanh located on a plateau about 30 minutes flying time west of DaNang. For two and a half months, beginning in late January, 1968, the enemy pounded the base continually with artillery and mortars and made numerous infantry probing attacks in an attempt to overrun the 6,000 American Marines who, along with a small number of South Vietnamese Army troops, were stationed there. General Giap invested roughly three North Vietnamese infantry divisions in this venture.[26]

Air power's response to the communist attack at Khe Sanh involved traditional missions—interdiction, close air support, airlift—all under the command and control of the 7th Air Force. Alarmed at the buildup of troops in the Khe Sanh area, General Momyer directed more than 20,000 attack sorties during December 1967 and January and February 1968 against communist lines of communication leading to the forces. More than 3,000 trucks supplying North Vietnamese forces were destroyed in this effort. Interdiction was crucial because the enemy counted on a high consumption attack to soften the defenses and destroy morale at Khe Sanh.[27]

Close air support was provided by fighters from the Air Force, Marines, and Navy Task Force 77 off the coast of Vietnam. Each day, 350 tactical fighters and 60 B–52s struck the enemy. To effect the command and control of this many aircraft in the confines of the valley where Khe Sanh was situated was a major feat. To meet this challenge, control of tactical air units of all services was centralized under 7th Air Force, making General Momyer the single manager for air for this particular battle. During the two and a half months of combat in that tiny area, more than 24,000 tactical and 2,700 B–52 sorties were flown, and more than 110,000 tons of bombs were dropped. During darkness, AC–47 gunships provided constant gunfire and illumination against enemy troops.[28]

The B–52s struck enemy staging, assembly, storage areas, and known gun positions. When communist troops were discovered digging trenches and tunnels to protect their advancing infantry, the B–52s bombed their positions, some within 1000 feet of the base perimeter. The weather was Hanoi's ally during this campaign; more than half of the fighter strikes and all of the B–52 strikes were controlled by Air Force radar.[29]

Another major air effort at Khe Sanh was the aerial resupply of the 6000 defenders. The runway at Khe Sanh was put out of operation by enemy artillery early in the siege. Therefore, for most of the period, the Air Force supplied Khe Sanh by airdrop and low-level cargo extraction missions. During the siege, the Air Force delivered more than 12,000 tons of supplies to Khe Sanh while under constant enemy fire. Supply levels at the fire base remained above the danger level because of the air lifeline.[30]

General Giap's forces suffered terribly, losing probably 10,000 killed. Two of his divisions were driven out of the war for the remainder of the American involvement.[31] Activities at Khe Sanh punctuated the lesson General Giap must have learned during the Tet offensive—that he could not conquer South Vietnam so long as American ground forces supported by air power remained.

Regardless of the important role air power played in thwarting General Giap's plans for 1968, the political climate in the United States had become so poisoned by the length and apparent futility of the war that President Johnson withdrew from the presidential campaign of 1968. The new President, Richard Nixon, announced less than six months after taking office his plan to withdraw United States combat troops from Vietnam. Fighting a drawn-out, apparently pointless war was unacceptable to the American public; 69,000 American troops were withdrawn from Vietnam—somewhat more than 10 percent of the total.[32]

The Air Force continued to support military operations in South Vietnam and kept up its attempt to interdict enemy lines of communication. In President Nixon's first year, B–52s struck time and time again at enemy concentrations, staging areas and fortifications to prevent the enemy from massing while American forces withdrew and South Vietnamese forces expanded. In the last five weeks of 1969, B–52s dropped more than 30 million pounds of bombs on enemy positions.[33]

In 1970, in keeping with President Nixon's withdrawals, the first United States Air Force elements began to leave Southeast Asia while the South Vietnamese Air Force enlarged its force structure. By the end of 1971, the Air Force had reduced its combat aircraft in South Vietnam to 177 (from a high in June 1968 of 737), with similar reductions of aircraft stationed in Thailand, the Philippines, and Okinawa. The number of Air Force people in South Vietnam itself also declined from the peak in 1968 of 54,434 to 28,791. By the end of the year, 70 percent of all air combat operations were being performed by the South Vietnamese Air Force.[34]

AIR POWER AND THE SPRING 1972 INVASION

1972 saw some of the most dramatic uses of air power in the entire war. United States Air Force and Navy air elements returned to the theater with dramatic vengeance in the spring of 1972 to retaliate against North Vietnam's attempt to conquer South Vietnam in a mass invasion.

The Spring 1972 invasion was a better planned and manned attack than the 1968 Tet offensive. General Giap committed 14 regular North Vietnamese divisions in attacks across the demilitarized zone, the central highlands, and the Cambodian border.[35] The attack began soon after midnight on March 30 with a massive artillery barrage and armored assault across the DMZ. Giap used hundreds of tanks and the largest mobile artillery pieces in his inventory to smash everything barring the way to Quang Tri City.

American military manpower in Vietnam at the end of March 1972 stood at 95,000, less than 20 percent of the peak of three years before, with the heaviest reductions having been taken by Army and Marine combat forces. It appeared that the South Vietnamese Army and Air Force would have to shoulder the brunt of the attack, as they had, in fact, been supplying most of the combat power in South Vietnam in the previous months. However, it became obvious within hours that the South Vietnamese could not defend against Giap's entire army, and President Nixon decided to provide massive reinforcement for the South Vietnamese in the form of air power.

On hand when the invasion began were 285 United States Air Force fighters, and 28 gunships in Vietnam and Thailand, 52 B–52s in Thailand, and a small number of C–130s and C–123s in Vietnam. More than 100 crucial American forward air controller aircraft also remained to help conduct operations. At the time of the invasion, the Navy also had two aircraft carriers off the coast of Vietnam with a total of about 180 strike aircraft.[36]

Intelligence concerns had led the United States to build up its B–52 force— the aircraft most feared by the communists—more than a month before the invasion. Some had been sent to Thailand, but the bulk had been deployed to Guam. Twenty-nine B–52s were in place on Guam at the time Giap invaded, and twenty more were sent four days later. By the time the invasion had been stopped, another 100 had been deployed to Guam. During the month of April, B–52s flew 1,600 sorties against the communists in South Vietnam and an additional 200 against communist lines of communication elsewhere.[37]

Hanoi, according to captured documents, believed antiwar sentiment in the United States would preclude any strong reaction to the invasion. Rapid battlefield victories causing major losses in the remaining American Army and Air Force units would force a precipitous United States withdrawal that would destroy the

Vietnamization program and undermine Nixon's stature at home during the election campaign.[38]

But, in fact, the President disregarded the antiwar movement and rapidly redeployed air and naval assets to the theater. The first Air Force and Marine fighters to arrive came from other bases in Korea, the Philippines, and Japan. The Navy responded rapidly, adding four aircraft carriers to Task Force 77; the first two arriving on the 3rd and 8th of April, the third arriving on the 30th of the month, and the last arrived later because it was redeployed from the Atlantic.[39] The Air Force Tactical Air Command in the United States also responded rapidly.

The first priority for the U.S. response was to help the South Vietnamese ground forces stabilize the ground situation. The massive force of B–52s and fighters already in the region were used to frustrate General Giap's hope for a rapid collapse of South Vietnam.[40]

The most difficult attack to deal with was the one in the northernmost region. Although tanks and armored vehicles were used in all phases of the invasion, the number involved in the attack across the demilitarized zone was especially heavy. About 400 armored vehicles supported at least 40,000 troops in this offensive. Additionally, this invading force brought with it mobile 130 mm artillery pieces.[41] Supply of the attacking army, moreover, was a simple matter for Hanoi. Perhaps General Giap hoped to sever the northern portion of South Vietnam from Saigon's control if he could not conquer the entire country.

Initially the attack in the north met weak resistance; in fact, the newly formed South Vietnamese Third Division broke early in the campaign. American C–130s rapidly moved elite South Vietnamese paratroopers and marines into Military Region I to try to stem Giap's attack. Nonetheless, by April 2 all twelve South Vietnamese fire support bases between Quang Tri City and the demilitarized zone had been captured, and the Communists were rapidly moving on the city itself.[42]

But General Giap did not have it all his way. American air power went to work early in April destroying the bridges over the My Chanh River, complicating Giap's logistic support to his forces, and many sorties were devoted to destroying the equipment abandoned by the South Vietnamese. Apparently wanting a quick victory, Giap moved his forces in daylight, even in clear weather! Convoys of heavy tanks and artillery moved down the roads exposed to air attack. American and Vietnamese air power hit these targets, striking first the 130 mm artillery, next the tanks, followed by the smaller artillery and, last, the trucks.[43]

The high priority assigned to the extremely accurate and long-range 130 mm artillery was because of its lethality. It was especially frightening to Vietnamese foot soldiers. Destroying the guns was fairly easy once they were located, but finding the guns had usually been difficult because the North Vietnamese were masters of camouflage, and this weapon was towed by tracked vehicles capable of traversing the most difficult terrain. Giap, moving on roads in daylight, now forfeited this advantage. Air Force fighters dropping laser-guided munitions were especially effective against these destructive weapons.[44]

The North Vietnamese had seldom used tanks in the past, so their introduction at this point in the war came as a major surprise. The Air Force used laser-guided 2000- or 3000-pound bombs to destroy many of them, and even more were destroyed by 500-pound general purpose bombs (simply because so many of these were dropped). The Vietnamese Army found that their Mark 48 tank was a worthy opponent to the North Vietnamese T–54 and PT–76 tank and used them in this manner. But because they lacked enough tanks in Military Region I, General Creighton Abrams, General Westmoreland's successor as MACV, requested the emergency airlift of six United States Mark 48s. Six giant United States C–5s brought the tanks and their crews into DaNang, and the crews drove off the ramp of the C–5s directly into the war.[45]

The application of air power in Military Region I had been massive. Friendly tactical fighters flew about 18,000 sorties in the three months beginning in April, with the United States Air Force providing 45 percent of those missions, the United States Navy and Marines (combined) about 30 percent, and the South Vietnamese the remaining 25 percent. Additionally, the Air Force B–52s flew some 2,700 sorties in that region. The Navy lost 2 aircraft; the Marines, 1; the Air Force, 20; and the South Vietnamese, 10. Air power played a key, even dominant, role in efforts to stop the communist assault. By the end of June, the exhausted remnants of Giap's northern forces were pushed back into the de-militarized zone.[46]

The communist offensive in Military Region III, surrounding Saigon, began three days after the attacks in Military Region I, after major South Vietnamese combat units had been shifted to the northern military regions. Apparently, Hanoi hoped to establish a provisional government at An Loc, on the Cambodian border, and then to move on Saigon itself. At least three North Vietnamese and one Viet Cong division were used in this attack, aided by massive antiaircraft artillery. The allies responded immediately with A–37s from Bien Hoa, naval tactical air from the USS *Constitution*, Vietnamese F–5s and A–1s, and Air Force F–4s and AC–130s from Thailand. Around-the-clock tactical air coverage was maintained over enemy forces from the earliest part of the attack. South Vietnamese infantry gave ground very stubbornly, but the communists were able to advance.[47]

Making a strategic stand, the Thieu government moved a large number of elite troops—rangers, paratroopers, and President Thieu's presidential guard—into An Loc to hold the city. Thus, by mid-April, five tough South Vietnamese regiments were inside the city, and the force was under attack by four enemy divisions that had seized both of the town's airfields. During the following two months, the South Vietnamese lacked surface logistics and depended upon the air for both firepower and supplies. Conditions in a siege are always ugly, and An Loc was no different; but air resupply kept the city alive.

Initially, after the enemy's seizure of the airfields at An Loc and Quan Loi in early April, the Army and the Vietnamese Air Force tried to sustain the city with helicopters. This effort was given up on 12 April because enemy fire destroyed so many vulnerable helicopters. The Vietnamese Air Force tried to airdrop to the city, but the ground fire was so intense the effort was abandoned by the 19th of April. United States Air Force C–130s were then used on a full-time basis. The usual drop altitude and airspeeds for supply drops made the C–130s too vulnerable to the intense antiaircraft artillery and ground fire in the area, and different techniques were employed in order to successfully sustain the city. The drop altitude was raised progressively to get the C–130s out of the range of ground fire, but as the altitude went up, accuracy of drops diminished. After two losses, the C–130s switched to night drops. The major drop zone available was a soccer field only about 2,000 meters square. Trying to hit this field consistently in daytime had been a challenge; at night, it was impossible. The defenders recovered less than a third of the loads, and the C–130s continued to be hit (one was lost and 37 others were damaged).

Air Force and Army troubleshooters, working feverishly at Saigon's Tan Son Nhut Air Base to improve the airdrop techniques, finally developed a tactic of dropping the loads well above 6,000 feet and electronically delaying parachute opening until just before impact. Using this new technique, the recovery rate reached more than 90 percent within a week. During the An Loc campaign from April 9 to May 10, the airlift forces flew 448 missions and dropped almost 3,700 tons of supplies to the beleaguered defenders. During the entire period of the siege (which ended on June 18), C–130s dropped 7,600 tons in more than 600 sorties.[48]

Realizing that the air resupply could make it impossible for them to force a surrender, the enemy elected to make a mass attack beginning on May 11. Artillery softening began on May 9. Captured enemy soldiers had given American commanders invaluable advance information, and the air forces were fully ready for the attack when it came. B–52s arrived every 55 minutes for 30 hours. The Air Force allocated 297 fighter-bombers to strike the enemy on May 11, and 260 sorties were allotted for each of the next three days. The Marines also sent 34 fighter-bombers to Bien Hoa to join in the campaign. The B–52s struck in three-ship cells with each aircraft dropping thirty tons of bombs, covering areas that would have required sixty fighter-bombers; these were especially effective.[49] By June 12 the enemy was driven from An Loc and the surrounding area by the viciousness of constant air attacks. There is no doubt that this battle would have been lost without air support.

North Vietnam's spring invasion, with its 14 divisions and 600 tanks, was frustrated by the tenacity of South Vietnamese ground forces and air power—mainly American. The Air Force, Navy, and Marines had rapidly moved potent forces into the theater to thwart General Giap's plans. Air power interdicted enemy lines of communication, destroyed communist infantry and armor in the field, and resupplied beleaguered friendly troops.

STRATEGIC BOMBING

The 1972 spring invasion had come in the midst of the (to that point) fruitless Paris negotiations that had begun in mid–1968. Antagonized by Hanoi's all-out spring attacks, and wanting to force North Vietnam out of the war,[50] the Nixon Administration decided to strike near the heart of North Vietnam with B–52s.[51] Their general misuse in the long war is reflected in the final statistics of B–52 missions. More than 124,500 B–52 sorties each dropped about 30 tons of bombs on targets in Indochina. But during the entire war, only 6 percent of these bombs were on North Vietnam, and the vast majority of that 6 percent was on targets far south of the heart of the country, Hanoi-Haiphong.[52]

On May 8, President Nixon announced the beginning of a comprehensive campaign against North Vietnam. The idea was to stem the flow of supplies into North Vietnam from its communist allies, to destroy existing stockpiles in North Vietnam, and to reduce markedly the flow of materials from Hanoi south. The campaign was called Operation *Linebacker*, and it went on simultaneously with the heavy fighting in South Vietnam. The campaign began with Operation *Pocket Money*, the mining of Haiphong and other major coastal points. On May 10, Nixon released almost all of the original 94 targets in North Vietnam for attack. Simultaneously, the President sharply reduced the no-bomb zones around Hanoi and Haiphong that had been established during the Johnson administration. With its spring offensive frustrated and now faced with extensive destruction in its own homeland, Hanoi indicated that it was interested in serious peace negotiations. With that signal, Nixon, in October, stopped the bombing of North Vietnam above the 20th parallel, expecting rapid progress would be made in the ongoing Paris negotiations.[53]

But once again the North Vietnamese showed their stubbornness. At home they rapidly moved supplies south; at the peace table in Paris they stalled, again testing the will of the American negotiators and people. Later in the fall, Hanoi actually withdrew from the peace talks altogether. The President determined that a very strong American response was warranted. On December 18, 1972, he called for an all-out air campaign against Vietnam's heartland to force a settlement that would permit the United States to withdraw. The interest was no longer interdiction nor to demonstrate that the North Vietnamese could not win in South Vietnam, but rather to so severely damage Hanoi's ability to wage war that the enemy would have to come to terms.

For the first time since the war had begun, strategic air power was employed with the determination that had all along been advocated by United States Air Force commanders. Over an eleven-day period between December 18 and 29, with a pause for Christmas Day, more than 700 B–52 sorties struck strategic targets in North Vietnam. This campaign, named *Linebacker* II, motivated the North Vietnamese to conclude the settlement that the United States had been seeking for years.[54]

B–52s were not the only aircraft involved in the Linebacker campaigns. In fact, more fighters than bombers flew against Hanoi and Haiphong. Fighter-bombers struck enemy airfields and some strategic targets, fighters flew against enemy interceptor aircraft, special fighter-bombers struck enemy radar and surface-to-air missile sites, other fighters dispensed chaff to confuse enemy radars, and other aircraft jammed enemy radars. Additionally, more than 200 KC-135 tankers refueled the B-52s between Guam and their targets in North Vietnam, a distance of more than 2,600 miles. The B-52s, along with the fighters that were involved, demanded about 750 refuelings each day of the campaign.[55]

To suppress the defenses, specific enemy airfields and radar sites had to be disabled shortly before the bombers arrived. The success of these efforts in support of the B-52 crews is reflected in the bomber loss rate of only 2 percent, against possibly the best defended target complex in history. Not London nor Ploesti nor Berlin during World War II had the defenses as sophisticated as the Hanoi-Haiphong area in 1972.[56]

The damage inflicted by the Guam and Thailand-based B-52s (and by fighter-bombers striking at other times of the day) was crippling. The Gia Lam railroad yard and repair facilities, the Bac Mai barracks, 80 percent of North Vietnam's electrical power production, and 25 percent of its petroleum stores were destroyed. Two days before the end of the campaign, all organized air defense in North Vietnam ceased; surface-to-air missile firing became spasmodic and aimless, and both B-52s and fighter aircraft roamed over North Vietnam at will. The country had been laid open for terminal destruction, and the North Vietnamese had to do something to avoid that eventuality. The result was that Hanoi quickly came to terms, and the President accepted. A number of aircrews however could not understand: "Why are we stopping now?" they asked.[57] At least one prominent analyst has pondered the same question.

Sir Robert Thompson, a leading authority on low-intensity conflict and the key strategist in the defeat of the Malayan communist insurgency, has argued that the bombing effort should not have been stopped when the North Vietnamese came to terms. If the goal was to drive North Vietnam *completely* out of the war so that the South Vietnamese could handle the insurgents and rebuild the country, the time to do that was after Hanoi's defenses were depleted.[58] Douglas Pike, one of the premier authorities in the West on North Vietnam, believed that the North Vietnamese were truly shocked by *Linebacker II* and has written: "Had a similar campaign of all-out bombing been made in early 1965," Lyndon Johnson probably could have achieved his goal of moving Hanoi's forces out of South Vietnam.[59] Although Hanoi would have maintained its objective of unifying Vietnam, they would have had to reassess the wisdom of seeking that goal through violence. The experience of the Korean war suggests an analogy. Massive bombing in the spring of 1953, on a scale never before experienced by the North Koreans and Chinese, forced a long truce—one that continues to this day—and has allowed the people governed by Seoul to prosper. But such was not to be the case in Vietnam.

Soon the war in Vietnam was over for the United States, and all American forces were withdrawn. The United States had misapplied air power from one end of the war to the other. Even the 11-day campaign of December 1972—a tactical success—stopped far short of fundamental goals. Losses to the United States over the period from the early 1960s to the early 1970s were staggering:

2,561 fixed-wing aircraft lost and 3,587 helicopters lost to hostile action (3,720 fixed-wing aircraft and 4,869 helicopters were lost altogether in connection with the war).[60] These losses could have been significantly reduced had President Johnson and Robert McNamara or President Nixon and Henry Kissinger used air power to its fullest potential. More important yet, South Vietnam might have survived. Little more than two years after *Linebacker II*, Hanoi, in flagrant violation of the January 1973 Paris peace settlement that brought them relief from the strategic bombing, swept across the demilitarized zone with 15 fresh divisions, penetrated deep into South Vietnam along the Laotian and Kampuchean borders, and as the poorly supported ARVN divisions panicked, quickly crushed South Vietnam. In the Spring of 1975, with no American air or ground power to counter this naked aggression and a rapidly dwindling U.S. supply effort to Saigon, Hanoi was finally victorious.

ACKNOWLEDGEMENTS

The author warmly thanks the many people who assisted him in shaping this manuscript. He received enormous help from several military and civilian historians and colleagues. Colonel John Sullivan read and criticized the manuscript several times, as did Robert Perry, Lieutenant Colonel Donald Baucom, Wayne Thompson, Colonel Tim Kline, Colonel Fred Shiner, Brigadier General Shirley (Sam) Carpenter, Lieutenant Colonel Craig Lamkin, and Captain Deborah Ferree. The author bears full responsibility, of course, for the themes and interpretations in the chapter, but he recognizes the contributions in correcting facts and smoothing language by the above. The author also most appreciated the stenographic, typing, and documentation abilities of Glenna Hughes without whose help the manuscript would not have been completed.

NOTES

1. There is a whole body of literature now gathering dust in libraries on successful counterinsurgencies. Twenty years ago, the Rand Corporation seriously studied this form of warfare and made major contributions to understanding its nature. Readers can refer to A. H. Peterson, et al., and their series—*Symposium on the Role of Airpower in Counterinsurgencies in Unconventional Warfare* (Santa Monica: Rand Corporation, [1964]); *Symposium on Airpower: The Algerian War* [1963]; *Symposium on Airpower: The Malaysian Emergency* [1964]; *Symposium on Airpower: The Philippines Huk Campaign*, [1963].

2. David Fromkin and James Chase in "What *Are* the Lessons of Vietnam?" *Foreign Affairs* (Spring 1985) p. 725, acknowledge that the Joint Chiefs of Staff saw the war more clearly than the "National Security Council and other civilian bodies."

3. Robert F. Futrell, *Advisory Years*, (Washington, D.C.: U.S. Government Printing Office, 1983), pp. 195–206.

4. William W. Momyer, *Air Power in Three Wars*, eds. A.J.C. Lavalle and J. C. Gaston, (Washington, D.C.: U.S. Government Printing Office, 1978), p. 13.

5. Momyer, *Air Power*, pp. 13–14.

6. Momyer, *Air Power*, p. 15.

7. Leslie H. Gelb and Richard K. Betts, *The Irony of Vietnam: The System Worked,* (Washington, D.C.: The Brookings Institution, 1979), pp. 101, 114–115; Momyer, *Air Power*, pp. 15–16.

8. Gelb and Betts, *The Irony of Vietnam*, p. 137; Momyer, *Air Power*, p. 17.

9. Gelb and Betts, *The Irony of Vietnam*, pp. 136–137.

10. U.S. Department of Defense, *United States–Vietnam Relations 1945–1967, IV. C. 7(a), Volume 1,* "The Air War in North Vietnam," The Pentagon Papers (Washington, D.C.: U.S. Government Printing Office, 1971), p. 5. (Hereafter *Pentagon Papers.*)

11. Gelb and Betts, *The Irony of Vietnam*, p. 136; Momyer, *Airpower*, pp. 18–19.

12. Momyer, *Air Power*, p. 19.

13. Gelb and Betts, *The Irony of Vietnam*, p. 138. General Momyer resented the proscriptions on attacks on North Vietnam airfields, surface-to-air missiles, and antiaircraft artillery sites. The costs were terrible. Momyer, *Air Power*, pp. 338–339.

14. Momyer, *Air Power*, p. 20.

15. Gelb and Betts, *The Irony of Vietnam*, pp. 53, 140; Armitage, M. J., and Mason, R. A., *Air Power in the Nuclear Age*, (Chicago: University of Illinois Press, 1983), p. 85; Pentagon Papers, IV. C. 7.(a), Vol. 1, pp. 1–6. Colonel Harry Summers called McNamara's bombing halts "fatal flaws" in the strategy. See Harry G. Summers, Jr., *On Strategy: The Vietnam War in Context* (Carlisle Barracks, Pa.: Army War College, 1983), p. 72.

16. *Pentagon Papers*, IV. C. 7.(a), Vol. 1. pp. 33–39. John T. McNaughton was a lawyer and a newspaper columnist. Unquestionably bright (a Rhodes Scholar), he had been a lawyer and professor for more than a decade before joining the Department of Defense as an attorney and as an Assistant Secretary of Defense in International Security Affairs. Although he had served in the Naval Reserves during World War II, there is nothing in his background or writing that indicates he had even scant knowledge of air power. McNaughton was apparently chief among McNamara's advisors counseling skepticism about bombing. He argued continually that bombing in South Vietnam would be more effective than bombing in North Vietnam and, by mid–1967, he had become so alarmed by the growing public protest against the war that he counseled President Johnson to rethink the entire premise of the war itself. He argued all along that there was no way the air war against North Vietnam could force Hanoi to abandon its war in the South. The Air Force did agree that at the levels Johnson and McNamara allowed, there was no way. *Who Was Who in America (With World Notables),* vol. iv. (Chicago: A. N. Marquis Co., n.d.) p. 646; Nelson Lichtenstein, ed. *Political Profiles: The Johnson Years,* (New York: Facts on File, Inc., n.d.), p. 395.

17. *Pentagon Papers*, IV. C. 7.(a), Vol. 1, pp. 17–19.

18. Momyer, *Air Power*, pp. 22–23.

19. Gelb and Betts, *The Irony of Vietnam*, p. 147. In 1966 the Central Intelligence Agency called for a drastically heightened air campaign in North Vietnam to drive Hanoi out of the war. Ibid., pp. 249–250.

20. Momyer, *Air Power*, pp. 10–11, 20–21; Armitage and Mason, *Air Power in the Nuclear Age*, p. 93; Carl Berger, ed., *The United States Air Force in Southeast Asia* (Washington, D.C.: U.S. Government Printing Office, 1977), pp. 11–13.

21. Gelb and Betts, *The Irony of Vietnam*, pp. 118–119; Berger, *Air Force in Southeast Asia*, pp. 40–41.

22. Berger, *Air Force in Southeast Asia*, pp. 47–52.

23. Momyer, *Air Power*, p. 313.

24. Berger, *Air Force in Southeast Asia*, p. 176; Momyer, *Air Power in Three Wars*, p. 319.

25. Momyer, *Air Power in Three Wars*, p. 318; Berger, *Air Force in Southeast Asia*, p. 56.

26. Berger, *Air Force in Southeast Asia*, pp. 52, 56; Armitage and Mason, *Air Power in the Nuclear War*, pp. 97–98; Momyer, *Air Power*, pp. 309–310.

27. Momyer, *Air Power*, pp. 307–308.

28. Ibid., p. 310; Berger, *Air Force in Southeast Asia*, pp. 52–56.

29. Berger, *Air Force in Southeast Asia*, pp. 151–157; Momyer, *Air Power*, p. 310.

30. Bernard C. Nalty, *Air Power and the Fight for Khe Sanh* (Washington, D.C.: Office of Air Force History, 1973), pp. 28–31, 103–105; Berger, *Air Force in Southeast Asia*, pp. 175–176.

31. Momyer, *Air Power*, pp. 310–311.

32. Berger, *Air Force in Southeast Asia*, p. 61.

33. Ibid., pp. 61–64.

34. Ibid.

35. Douglas Pike, ''The Other Side,'' in *Vietnam as History: Ten Years After the Paris Accords*, ed. Peter Braestrup, (Washington: University Press of America, 1984), p. 76.

36. John A. Doglione et al., *Airpower and the 1972 Spring Invasion*, USAF Southeast Asia Monograph Series, vol. ii, monograph 3 (Washington: U.S. Government Printing Office, 1976), pp. 14, 12, 31.

37. Ibid., pp. 26–29.

38. Ibid., p. 29.

39. Ibid., pp. 15–16.

40. Momyer, *Air Power*, p. 32.

41. Armitage and Mason, *Air Power in the Nuclear Age*, pp. 87, 98–99.

42. Ibid.; Pike, ''The Other Side,'' in *Vietnam as History*, p. 76; Doglione et al., *Spring Invasion*, pp. 4, 46; Momyer, *Air Power*, pp. 32, 328.

43. Doglione et al., *Spring Invasion*, pp. 51, 53.

44. Ibid., pp. 53–54; Momyer, *Air Power*, pp. 327–328.

45. Doglione et al., *Spring Invasion*, pp. 54–56.

46. Ibid., p. 58; Momyer, *Air Power*, pp. 328–329.

47. Momyer, *Air Power*, p. 330; Doglione et al., *Spring Invasion*, pp. 78–80.

48. Doglione et al., *Spring Invasion*, pp. 92–98.

49. Berger, *Air Force in Southeast Asia*, pp. 182–183; Doglione et al., *Spring Invasion*, pp. 92–98, 98–104; Momyer, *Air Power*, pp. 332–333.

50. Armitage and Mason, *Air Power in the Nuclear Age*, pp. 99–100; Fromkin and Chase in *Foreign Affairs*, p. 738; and Pike, ''The Other Side,'' in *Vietnam as History*, p. 76.

51. Doglione et al., *Spring Invasion*, pp. 105–106; Berger, *Air Force in Southeast Asia*, p. 65; Armitage and Mason, *Air Power in the Nuclear Age*, pp. 109–110; and Pike, ''The Other Side,'' in *Vietnam as History*, p. 76.

52. Berger, *Air Force in Southeast Asia*, p. 167.

53. Armitage and Mason, *Air Power in the Nuclear Age*, p. 88; and Momyer, *Air Power*, pp. 33–34.

54. Berger, *Air Force in Southeast Asia*, p. 166; Momyer, *Air Power*, pp. 33–34; Armitage and Mason, *Air Power in the Nuclear Age*, p. 88; Pike, "The Other Side," in *Vietnam as History*, p. 76.

55. James R. McCarthy and George B. Allison, *Linebacker II: A View from the Rock*, USAF Southeast Asia Monograph Series, vol. 6, monograph 8, (Washington, D.C.: U.S. Government Printing Office, 1979) pp. 139–140, 56.

56. Ibid., pp. 41–44, 68–70, 6–7.

57. Ibid., p. 172.

58. Sir Robert Thompson, "Rear Bases and Sanctuaries," in *The Lessons of Vietnam*, eds. W. Scott Thompson and Donaldson D. Frizzel (New York: Crane, Russak & Company, 1977), p. 105. Those Americans unfortunate enough to be on the ground in Hanoi saw directly the psychological impact of the raids on the North Vietnamese. They have testified to the dramatic change in the attitudes of the guards and the guards' supervisors. McCarthy and Allison, *Linebacker II*, pp. 174–175.

59. Pike, "The Other Side," in *Vietnam as History*, p. 72.

60. Office of the Assistant Secretary of Defense, Comptroller, *Southeast Asia Statistical Summary*, Washington, D.C., 1973, Table 350A. Armitage and Mason, *Air Power in the Nuclear Age*, pp. 112–113, from slightly different numbers.

5

Earl H. Tilford, Jr.

Air Power in Vietnam: The Hubris of Power

More than a decade has passed since the last helicopters pulled away from the rooftop of the United States Embassy in Saigon. Their departure marked the end of American involvement in a conflict that spanned a generation, costing 57,000 American lives and nearly two hundred billion dollars. In the nearly fifteen years of the war, the U.S. Air Force lost 2,257 aircraft, suffered, 5,578 casualties, including 2,118 deaths, with several hundred airmen still listed as missing in action.[1] During the war, American political and military leaders made many mistakes, and blame for our ultimate defeat can be shared in many quarters.

The U.S. Army, perhaps because it suffered the most in Vietnam, began analyzing what went wrong back in the early 1970s. By contrast, the U.S. Air Force has made little effort to learn from its Vietnam experiences. For instance, from 1974 to 1979, the Air War College curriculum included only a 2.5 hour case study of *Linebacker* operations entitled ''TACAIR in Vietnam,'' comprising 1.4 percent of the 172 hours in the segment of instruction devoted to studying the use of general purpose forces.[2] Indeed, the word *Vietnam* appears in neither the 1979 nor the vastly improved 1984 versions of Air Force Manual 1–1, *Basic Aerospace Doctrine of the United States Air Force*.[3]

The Air Force has not paid enough attention to the Vietnam War for a number of reasons. To begin with, top Air Force commanders believed that we had, indeed, won the war . . . or could have won it had ''restraints'' not been imposed.[4] Then, in the years immediately following the 1973 cease-fire that allowed for U.S. withdrawal, there was a concerted effort to ''put Vietnam behind us'' as we returned to preparing for the next war which, presumably, would have air power used according to the strategic principles that worked so well in World War II. This attitude was not new. Following the Korean War, the Air Force chose to regard that conflict as a never-to-be-repeated diversion from the true course of strategic air power and, therefore, not worthy of extensive analysis. The lessons that might have been learned in Korea could have proved useful in

Vietnam just as the lessons to be learned from Vietnam should have applicability in some future limited but protracted war.

ASKING THE RIGHT QUESTIONS

Today, diversions to deal with terrorism notwithstanding, planning for war is focused on building forces that can fight a conventional or nuclear war in Europe or that can deploy rapidly to areas as diverse as the Middle East, Central America, or Korea. Additionally, issues concerned with fighting a war in space are also emerging. In the Air Force, the emphasis is on acquiring the kind of sophisticated weapons that enhance our "preparedness" with the predominant question remaining: "How do you fight outnumbered and win?"

This might be the wrong question, though. For instance, it is easy to understand how ten men armed with automatic rifles can defeat a hundred men armed with spears. Even today, despite dramatic gains in the last few years, American forces would probably have a technological edge over Soviet opponents in an armed conflict. Military thinkers should, however, look at warfare in its wider context, going beyond numbers of weapons, divisions, and sizes of air and sea fleets to include such factors as firepower, reliability of weapons, logistical support (or lack thereof) for sustaining the military in battle, technical competence of people using the weapons, morale, and other such variables that determine the total military capability of an armed force. Above all, the Air Force needs to examine the lessons that are available from the Vietnam War.

Retired Army Colonel Harry G. Summers, Jr., argues in his book, *On Strategy: A Critical Analysis of the Vietnam War*, that the American military won virtually all the battles.[5] U.S. troops certainly outclassed the enemy in firepower and resources available for prosecuting the war. Nevertheless, American foreign-policy objectives were not realized and, in essence, the war was lost. However, instead of asking what the North Vietnamese and the Viet Cong did right and what the United States did wrong, too many American officers seemed content to blame antiwar activists, the press, and the liberal politicians for what happened. This kind of thinking, while perhaps containing an element of truth, has led to the development of a "our hands were tied" thesis that resembles the "stab in the back" theories that plagued the German military after World War I and the French generals after the German victory in June 1940.

Perhaps the questions should be: "Did the North Vietnamese, rather than the United States, have a better understanding of the complex nature of modern warfare?" Basic strategy courses teach that war is more than a contest between armed forces. It is a struggle between nations that incorporates economic, cultural, social, and political, as well as military, dimensions. The North Vietnamese knew they were militarily outclassed from the beginning, but their success was derived from developing a strategy that exploited American weaknesses in other areas. Throughout the war, the United States relied on an attrition strategy that employed massive firepower and technological superiority in an attempt to bend the enemy to its will. While those who planned and managed the war suffered from hubris by assuming that eventually our technological superiority would prevail, they also failed to give enough consideration to the varied costs and drawbacks of this strategy.

In the 1950s and early 60s, Americans generally believed that science was bringing mankind into a technological utopia. Advertisements of the era boasted that "progress is our most important product" and promised "better living through chemistry." In the Air Force, there was a commitment to flying and fighting in machines of unparalleled sophistication. The emphasis was very much on speed. The F–104 was "the missile with a man in it." The B–58 Hustler, capable of speeds in excess of Mach 2, was in the inventory of the Strategic Air Command. The XB–70, a bomber able to fly at nearly three times the speed of sound, was in development. Faith in technology, coupled with the certainty that air power had been decisive in ending the Second World War and would be decisive in any future conflicts, contributed to the hubris that plagued us in Vietnam.

The U.S. Air Force had been oriented toward technology from its birth; and, in the early sixties, just as American faith in progress dating from the nineteenth century seemed to peak, the Air Force positioned itself on the cutting edge of this new era. The term *aerospace* aptly described its ambitions—to fly and to fight, not only in the air, but in space also. *Aerospace* is a term that implies no inherent restrictions. Land has its limits and so do the oceans, but space, as an extension of the atmosphere, has none. Did our faith in technology dull our ability to perceive its shortcomings? As the United States moved toward military involvement in Indochina, most American officers had an unshakable faith in their undeniable superiority in military technology. We failed to understand that high technology carries with it significant constraints and costs in other areas.

Time proved to be one of those constraints. It was the enemy of the complex logistical systems required by sophisticated weapons. According to General William C. Westmoreland, commander of Military Assistance Command, Vietnam (MACV), from 1964–68, it took him three years to obtain the men to establish his transportation system and secure the bases he needed to go on the offensive against the Viet Cong in 1967.[6] It took Westmoreland these three years to build the logistic bases needed to support the kind of operations he wanted to carry out—airmobile assaults dependent on helicopters and armored personnel carriers. During these years, American forces suffered casualties and their frustrations increased as the war continually lacked clearly defined goals, producing few readily identifiable victories.[7] Furthermore, the time needed to get sufficient forces into Southeast Asia belied the term *limited war* because, after three years of increasing the commitment in numbers of men and amounts of material, the war could not be termed anything other than protracted. The United States should have heeded the ancient Chinese warrior-philosopher Sun Tzu's admonition: "Victory is the main object in war. If this is long delayed, weapons are blunted and morale depressed."[8] More recently, General George C. Marshall, U.S. Army

Chief of Staff in the Second World War, warned, "a democracy cannot fight a Seven Years' War."[9]

The North Vietnamese made use of time, turning it to their advantage. Within the Buddhist-Confucian scheme of things, time was cyclical, and without the strict, linear implications intrinsic to Western concepts. The Vietnamese had outlasted the French, and they were determined to endure the Americans as well because, after all, Vietnam was their homeland and the Americans would have to go home eventually. The Vietnamese reasoned that if they could avoid a military debacle, time would give them the advantage. Furthermore, the passage of time would multiply the effect of inflicting casualties on the Americans, ensuring that at some point the American public would tire of the war, just as the French public had tired of the earlier conflict.[10]

The Vietnamese also relied on our traditional disregard for history. While the French fought long and hard in Vietnam and suffered equivalently more casualties, the Americans learned little from them. The French military attaché in Saigon, in the early 60s, was told to provide the Americans with whatever advice and help he could make available. He received only one visit from an American during the first year and a half of his assignment and that American was a civilian defense contractor of French ancestry.[11] Likewise, General Westmoreland wrote that while he kept copies of most of Bernard Fall's works and Mao's "little red book on the theories of guerrilla warfare" beside his bed, "I was usually too tired in late evening to give the books more than occasional attention."[12]

Neither did the United States seem to have considered the inherent bureaucratic momentum that high technology and its supporting structures generate. Supplies had to be computer programmed into user organizations. Resources had to be consumed at the predetermined rate specified by managers. Furthermore, and perhaps the most difficult thing for an organization dedicated to researching, developing, and producing technologically sophisticated machines to do is to admit that these machines might be inappropriate for the task at hand.

This bureaucratic imperative made managers demand that resources either be used or lost. In the interdiction campaign, referred to as "Commando Hunt," against the Ho Chi Minh Trail, the effectiveness of air power was calculated by estimating the amount of enemy supplies arriving in South Vietnam as a fraction of those entering the supply pipeline from North Vietnam. According to General William W. Momyer, former Air Force commander in Vietnam, "The statistics were and are subject to differences of interpretation."[13] Without a doubt, the United States destroyed many trucks and kept a large quantity of supplies from reaching South Vietnam's battlefields. The use of AC–130 gunships, with their computer-aimed, 40-mm cannon and 105-mm howitzers, proved particularly innovative and successful.[14] Nevertheless, supplies got through and the degree of success achieved by air power remains subject to "differences of interpretation."

Despite the air campaigns against the infiltration corridors, the North Vietnamese were able to stockpile vast amounts of war material in the "Parrot's Beak" border area of Cambodia, west of Saigon, thus requiring an American incursion into the region in 1970. While a great deal of these supplies came into the "Parrot's Beak" across Cambodia from the port at Sihanoukville, much of it came down the Ho Chi Minh Trail.[15] The following year, 1971, the Army of the Republic of Vietnam (ARVN) marched to the center of the Ho Chi Minh Trail, the transhipment point at Tchepone, in an effort to cut the supply corridor and forestall a major enemy offensive against the northern part of South Vietnam.[16] Despite American bombing, the North Vietnamese Army in Laos routed the ARVN. Finally, in 1972, two years after the port at Sihanoukville had been closed to Communist ships, the North Vietnamese infiltrated enough troops, artillery, trucks, and even T–34, T–54, and T–55 tanks to launch a major invasion of South Vietnam. Although a definitive history of the Commando Hunt operations has yet to be written, it is likely that historians will conclude that this massive bombing campaign was not successful in inhibiting significantly the North Vietnamese war-making capability in the South.

In the Commando Hunt campaigns, the United States measured success by estimating the quantity of supplies stopped along the trail and in numbers of trucks destroyed or damaged. Perhaps American analysts should have assessed other costs in terms of money, effort, and effect on morale in determining the impact on the overall war effort. Each sortie meant more money spent on fuel and bombs. As sortie rates climbed, the wear on aircraft, especially B–52s, which, even at that time, were beginning to show their age, increased. Furthermore, national resolve was weakened when the secret bombings of Laos and Cambodia became public knowledge, and the American citizenry began to ask what contribution the dropping of high explosives on the Indochinese jungle was making toward the achievement of national goals in Southeast Asia.[17]

Aircraft losses, like the casualty count of American soldiers, had an adverse effect on the American public. Each day the evening newscasters duly reported the loss of American planes. After President Lyndon B. Johnson limited the bombing of North Vietnam on March 31, 1968 and then ended the Rolling Thunder campaign on November 1, many Americans assumed that our losses would decrease as wings of American fighters and bombers, presumably with less to do, would return home. However, because the bombing did not decrease but merely shifted across the Annamite Mountains to concentrate on the Ho Chi Minh Trail, sortie and loss rates did not go down. Enemy defenses along the Ho Chi Minh Trail intensified after 1968 as the North Vietnamese moved numerous antiaircraft guns into Laos. Surface-to-air missile (SAM) sites were placed just across the border inside North Vietnam where they were relatively safe from attacks from other than "protective reaction strikes."[18] By late 1968, enemy defenses along the infiltration corridors resembled those previously encountered in the Hanoi and Haiphong areas of North Vietnam. Air Force combat losses, totaling 421 in 1967 at the height of *Rolling Thunder*, continued at a high rate through 1968 at 392.[19] The continued cost in resources and lost lives had an adverse psychological and political effect in that it fueled the arguments of antiwar critics who were asking why this perceived waste was continuing.

WAR AND THE BUREAUCRATIC IMPERATIVE

Another example of bureaucratic inertia and technological inflexibility occurred near the end of the war. Air Force combat operations over North and South Vietnam ceased with the signing of the Paris peace accords in January 1973, but the bombing of Laos continued into April, and the bombing of Cambodia went on until Congress mandated an end to it on August 15. The air armada that had shortly before conducted massive operations over North Vietnam during *Linebacker I* and *II* was still, for the most part, in Southeast Asia. The "use it or lose it" imperative began to govern the employment of these air resources. For example, a fixed number of B–52 sorties was available every day for use in Southeast Asia. Through April 1973 these sorties were directed at Laos and Cambodia. After the bombing of Laos stopped in late spring, more B-52 sorties were available for use in Cambodia. It seemed that every one of these sorties had to be targeted somewhere, even if targets justifying a B–52 strike were not available. According to a former targeteer responsible for planning B–52 missions, the situation got so desperate that on some days he would direct a number of sorties against fictitious "underwater storage areas" in the Tonle Sap (a large lake) to reduce the chances of killing innocent Cambodians.[20] Again, every additional dollar spent, sortie flown, and bomb dropped became a weapon in the hands of those opposed to American policy in Southeast Asia.

Technology provided a multitude of options for the conduct of military operations. There were the "Igloo White" and "Task Force Alpha" sensor programs, the beginnings of the "electronic battlefield."[21] Advancements in weapons technology produced mini-mine area denial weapons, propane fuel-air explosives, and laser-guided bombs. While these weapons were quite often used effectively, one needs to ask if the sophisticated capabilities of the weapons and the abundance of resources made us too confident in our belief that the North Vietnamese would have to succumb to the overwhelming weight of American might.

Simply stated, one of the biggest mistakes that comprised the predominant part of our hubris was the presumption that victory would accrue through the use of high-tech weaponry and massive firepower without giving adequate consideration to devising a sound strategy. Air Force analysts searched for a quantifiable criterion that would signify victory. The sortie count, bomb damage assessments, killed-by-air figures, and truck counts constituted a seemingly endless list of compilations that indicated we were, by late 1967, slowly but surely winning a war of attrition.

Abundance and complexity necessitated management. During the Vietnam War, all the services, to varying extents, emphasized the arts and sciences of management. Military managers became like their civilian counterparts in the world of business in demanding empirical criteria for determining success or failure. In the financial world, indications of success or failure are commonly assessed through dollar figures that indicate profit or loss. In warfare, assessments of success or failure—victory or defeat—may not be so easy. Because there were few clearly definable objectives in the Vietnam War, such as cities to be captured or enemy frontiers to be penetrated, it was difficult to measure success. However, as is typically American, the military managers, like their civilian superiors, demanded ''progress.'' While doubts about the Vietnam War increased at home, the ''can do'' attitude prevailed in the Air Force. The Vietnam era was the period of ''Zero Defects'' and PRIDE—''Professional Results in Daily Efforts''—programs.[22] Further complicating the situation, officers and airmen found themselves in Southeast Asia for a limited tour of one year. Without strategic objectives, an assignment to Southeast Asia became a 365-day requirement to excel according to short-term management criteria. In an atmosphere that discouraged dissent and demanded conformity, and in a place where—by 1968, we had, in effect, lost the war—careerism and ''filling that square'' for promotion all too often supplanted a commitment to real professionalism. Those who bore the brunt of the injury caused by this condition were those who were, in essence, most innocent—the crews who flew the missions and who sometimes had to pay the ultimate price.

After the inauguration of President Nixon in January 1969, ''Vietnamization'' became American policy. In Madison Avenue parlance, Vietnamization meant quitting, indicating that the United States had accepted the notion that the war was unwinnable. No one wanted to be the last American killed in a losing cause. The importance of saving lives, despite the tactical or strategic consequences, increased and was evidenced by the Air Force's elaborate search and research (SAR) operations. Two SAR operations that took place late in the war are illustrative. In early December 1969 a massive rescue effort evolved to save the backseater of ''Boxer 22,'' an F–4 shot down near Tchepone, Laos, in the very center of the Ho Chi Minh Trail. During this operation, 336 sorties were flown, many by Air Force, Navy, and Marine fighter-bombers diverted from their original targets. Before the operation was successfully concluded, one pararescueman was killed, five of the ten HH–3 and HH–53 helicopters that received battle damage were so mangled that they had to be scrapped, and five A–1 single-engine propeller-driven rescue escort aircraft were severely damaged.[23] In another rescue operation that took place during the North Vietnamese 1972 spring offensive, tremendous efforts were made to save the lives of two American aviators. On April 2, 1972, an EB–66 twin-engine jet was shot down over the northern Quang Tri Province just south of the demilitarized zone. A lone survivor parachuted into the path of the advancing enemy army. For twelve days, the Air Force conducted a gigantic rescue operation for the downed airman, who was joined in evading the enemy by another airman shot down during the rescue attempt. As was usual in rescue attempts, strike aircraft were diverted from other missions to aid in the recovery efforts. Meanwhile, the North Vietnamese shot down two U.S. Army helicopters, an Air Force ''Jolly Green Giant'' rescue helicopter and an Air Force OV–10 observation aircraft. For nearly two weeks, the survivors avoided capture while MACV declared a ''no fire zone'' in the vicinity of the evading Americans; this meant that artillery could not fire into the area without prior clearance, a region which was also occupied by the invading North Vietnamese force. Meanwhile, the Army of the Republic of Vietnam's 3rd Division was being mauled by a vastly superior Communist force. American priorities at that time seemed to place stopping the North Vietnamese invasion below that of saving the lives of two aviators.[24]

Even if the success of Commando Hunt is open to question, air power can be judged a failure in *Rolling Thunder*, the longest single bombing campaign ever conducted by the U.S. Air Force, lasting from March 2, 1965 until October 31, 1968. The bombing had two objectives: first, to stop the flow of men and supplies from North Vietnam south, through the southern panhandle and then along the Ho Chi Minh Trail in Laos and down the coast; and second, to compel the North Vietnamese to stop supporting the Viet Cong and negotiate an end to the conflict.[25] *Rolling Thunder* failed to achieve these objectives.

Rolling Thunder failed for many reasons, but basically it was strategically flawed in that the United States tried to use conventional air power on North Vietnam to affect an unconventional war in the South. North Vietnam was an agricultural nation, and bombing its rudimentary industrial base and primitive transportation system simply did not have much effect.

Another reason for its failure was that although *Rolling Thunder* was extensive, it was also restrained. The numbers of sorties, targets, and even weapon loads were tightly controlled, at least through the first months, by the Office of the Assistant Secretary of Defense for International Security Affairs (ASD/ISA). While Seventh Air Force generated target lists through CINCPAC and the Joint Chiefs of Staff, ASD/ISA evaluated each target before sending the list to the White House for final review. There President Johnson, the Secretary of Defense, the Secretary of State, the President's Special Assistant for National Security Affairs, his press secretary, and, on occasion, the Chairman of the Joint Chiefs of Staff decided what targets should be struck. They even decided how many planes would go on each mission, the routes of ingress and egress, what weapons could or could not be used, and whether a restrike might be authorized.[26] Although President Johnson wanted the air attacks to ''send a message to Hanoi,'' if Ho Chi Minh got any message at all from this restraint, it was that the United States lacked the resolve to wage the war to a successful conclusion.[27]

Finally, and perhaps most important, there was enemy determination. The North Vietnamese had decided that they were not going to be defeated. If U.S. air strikes knocked down a bridge, hordes of peasants mobilized to repair the destruction caused by bombs, to build fords, or to put in an underwater bridge. The bombing may even have strengthened the resolve of a people who were culturally inured to adversity.[28]

Politically, nothing was more controversial than the *Rolling Thunder* campaign. To many Americans and the world community at large, it seemed as if a cruel and excessive technological force had been unleashed on a "peaceful and peace-loving people." The North Vietnamese milked this impression for all the propaganda value they could garner. Accordingly, the propaganda cost alone may have exceeded the military value of the bombing. Furthermore, the air attacks on North Vietnam saddled the United States with the albatross of aggression and allowed the Soviets and their allies to justify keeping North Vietnam supplied with arms for "self-protection."[29]

Tactically, Air Force, Navy, and Marine aircrews performed well. The bombing caused extensive damage to North Vietnam's military installations and its small industrial base. While the effort at shutting down the flow of men and supplies southward failed, the air strikes did wreak havoc with the rudimentary transportation network.[30] According to Department of Defense estimates, the United States reportedly destroyed or put out of commission 77 percent of North Vietnam's ammunition depots and 65 percent of its petroleum storage facilities. U.S. air forces dropped or seriously damaged 55 percent of their major bridges and destroyed an estimated 12,500 vessels, nearly 10,000 vehicles, and almost 2,000 rail cars along with a handful of locomotives in strikes and armed reconnaissance missions along their lines of communications. Our air strikes forced the mobilization of over half a million men and women to repair the transportation network and disperse their supply caches. Another 150,000 people were used to man antiaircraft guns, fire automatic weapons at attacking aircraft, and run bomb shelters.[31]

Most of the air-to-air action occurred during *Rolling Thunder*, but, even then, it was the exception rather than the rule. There were relatively few classic dogfights, and, throughout the war, the North Vietnamese relied on a combination of surface-to-air missiles, antiaircraft guns, and thousand of peasants, militia, and soldiers firing rifles and automatic weapons, rather than interceptors to effectively deny air superiority to the Americans. In air-to-air action, the Air Force, Navy, and Marines shot down enemy fighters at a rate of about 2.2 to 1. While this is not spectacular in comparison with, for instance, Israeli performances over the Bekka Valley, it is still a respectable kill-ratio.

However, our air-to-air performance bears a closer look because it has been touted as an indication of what superior technology can accomplish. Most of the aerial engagements took place over North Vietnam, with a few extending into northeastern Laos. Therefore, if, when a Vietnamese plane was shot down, its pilot was not killed by the initial trauma of being hit by a missile or gunfire, and, if he survived the ejection (which in some MiGs was not a foregone conclusion), he usually lived to fight another day. While the North Vietnamese did not have formal rescue and recovery units, we can assume that they were at least as proficient at finding their own airmen as they were at finding U.S. airmen shot down over North Vietnam.

On the other hand, when an American plane went down in air-to-air combat, it was almost always over enemy territory. Moreover, since the Air Force's air superiority fighter was the two-place F–4 Phantom, two airmen were at risk whenever a MiG won a fight with a Phantom. Although one's chances for rescue depended on many factors, including when in the war one was shot down and, of course, where. Overall, if shot down over North Vietnam, one's chance for rescue was one in six.[32]

Perhaps because of our dependence on technologically sophisticated weapons and a complex system of logistical support, we assumed that the Viet Cong and their North Vietnamese allies would suffer as much from supply interruptions, the destruction of fuel depots, and the loss of electrical power as the United States Army and Air Force would. That was not the case because the Communist forces fighting in South Vietnam between 1965 and 1968 were somewhere on the spectrum of warfare between guerilla and conventional in nature. The Viet Cong could live off the countryside, growing what food they did not take from peasants. They taxed the local population for dry goods as well as money. They took weapons from dead ARVN or American troops or purchased them on the black market. In 1967, at the height of their power, the Viet Cong could survive on an estimated 15 tons of supplies that reached them from North Vietnam each day. If, according to estimates made by the Central Intelligence Agency, you factor in the more conventional North Vietnamese regular forces operating inside South Vietnam in 1967, taken together, the Viet Cong and their North Vietnamese allies still needed only a total of 100 tons of supplies a day to sustain operations in a war that was, essentially, stalemated.[33]

A hundred tons sounds like alot of supplies, but it is, in fact, only 50 truck loads. The Ho Chi Minh Trail was 250 miles long, and it included an estimated 6,000 miles of roadways, pathways, streams, and rivers down which supplies could be moved. By no means did all supplies come south in trucks. Some were carried on the backs of porters or on bicycles. Fifty-five gallon drums were packed with supplies and floated down streams. And, a large portion of the supplies that reached South Vietnam came by water, through the Gulf of Tonkin, and into the Cambodian port of Sihanoukville, before that was lost to the Communists following the Lon Nol coup in Phnom Penh in March 1970. In effect, a hundred tons of supplies proved to be too small a trickle for air power to shut off.

THE MYTH OF LINEBACKER II

Air power enthusiasts point to *Linebacker II* as an example of independent bombing that reinforces the viability of strategic bombardment. Indeed, *Linebacker II*, the so called "Christmas Bombing" of December 1972 was a success, though with some qualifications. President Nixon ordered the bombing to compel the North Vietnamese to resume peace talks after they had walked out of the Paris negotiations in October. In *Linebacker II* the Air Force flew 740 B–52 sorties and the Air Force, Navy and Marines struck with about 1,200 fighter-bomber sorties to hit targets around and in North Vietnam's major cities. While B–52s struck railyards, supply depots, and petroleum storage facilities, F–4s, carrying laser-guided bombs, streaked to downtown Hanoi to destroy targets like the Hanoi power plant with surgical precision. This and similar targets had been off limits during *Rolling Thunder* because of American policy that demanded doing everything possible to limit collateral damage to civilian structures.[34]

Linebacker II has been surrounded by controversy and shrouded in myth. Given the antiwar climate of the time, Americans and most of the rest of the world were receptive to the suggestion that the bombing constituted another "Dresden" of "carpet bombing," entailing a "holocaust" that laid waste to the cities of North Vietnam.[35] North Vietnam's claim that it shotdown 34 B–52s and 49 or so fighter-bombers, while not accepted by most reputable historians, was, likewise, not dismissed for the propaganda rhetoric that it was.[36] Many in the Air Force have clung to the myth that *Linebacker II* was a great "fourth down play" that delivered us from defeat. As such, this line of reasoning has contributed to the "hands tied behind our back" theory that tends to dominate some postwar thinking in the Air Force.

In most myths kernels of truth can be found and the myths surrounding *Linebacker II* are no exception. Militarily, *Linebacker II* was a success. It paved the way for the United States to withdraw its forces from South Vietnam and compelled the North Vietnamese to return American prisoners of war. Still, withdrawals and the repatriation of POWs is not the stuff of which national victories are made. In the euphoria that accompanied the signing of the peace agreements, the final withdrawal of American troops, and the return of the prisoners of war, there was an illusion of victory. This illusion has fed the myth, prompting some Air Force officers, in the years since the end of American participation in the war, to voice the opinion that, "The Christmas bombings of 1972 should have taken place in 1965."[37] While it is tempting to accept the argument that had a *Linebacker II*-type operation been conducted in 1965, the war might have ended differently, there are many problems with this position. In 1965, the North Vietnamese would have had much to lose by ending the fighting. Perhaps they would have agreed to stop supporting the Viet Cong and respected the territorial integrity of the Republic of Vietnam, but for how long? The guerrilla war in the South would have, in all probability, continued because the Viet Cong, despite recent claims of the regime in Hanoi, had a life of its own and, in 1965, the National Liberation Front was still relatively independent of Hanoi, at least militarily. Furthermore, there is no reason to suspect that Hanoi would have respected any agreement signed in 1965 since it did not respect the Paris agreements of 1973. Additionally, in 1972, the United States primarily wanted what the French had sought in 1954—a way out of the war. The Communists, on the other hand, had much more fully attained their political and military goals—the withdrawal of American forces and the right to participate in the political process inside South Vietnam. With time as their ally, the North Vietnamese reasoned that after the Americans went home they would eventually win. In December 1972, with most of their military and political objectives realized—or at least realizable—it made good sense for the North Vietnamese to sign what was, in effect, a very beneficial peace agreement. In 1965, with American demands that also included the withdrawal of all North Vietnamese troops from South Vietnam (a condition that was not a part of the 1973 agreements), the North Vietnamese would have been very far from realizing their goals, and it is probable that they would not have agreed to what were, at that time and from their point of view, much less reasonable American conditions for peace.

After the North Vietnamese had launched virtually every surface-to-air missile in their inventory to shoot down fifteen B–52s and eight or nine fighter-bombers, and after we had wrecked their air defense system, they asked if the peace negotiations could be resumed. At that point, further resistance was futile and, in that North Vietnam was virtually defenseless, fraught with danger. By December 28, 1972, the eleventh day of the campaign, B–52s could fly over North Vietnam with relative impunity. While it is not clear exactly why North Vietnam asked for a resumption of the peace talks, certainly the bombing played a key role in prompting them to do so. Negotiations, when they resumed, moved ahead rapidly and, on January 23, 1973, the United States, North Vietnam, South Vietnam, and the National Liberation Front signed a cease-fire agreement.

CONCLUSION

Pride fosters hubris and, in our pride, the Vietnam War remains a very difficult one for the Air Force to assess. It is easy to point to *Linebacker II* as a vindication of independent bombing and press forward, oblivious to the difficulties and problems we experienced in other air operations. Why, for instance, did we continue to bomb North Vietnam, losing 990 American planes and spending better than six billion dollars to inflict about 600 million dollars in damage, when all the indications were that this bombing was not going to achieve the stated objectives? Why did we attack North Vietnam at ten in the morning, two in the afternoon, and again at four in what has been called "the Dr. Pepper War"? Was it because North Vietnam was most susceptible to our air strikes at those times or was it because maintenance routines generated sorties at a prescribed rate? Did we devise a suitable strategy for our air war against North Vietnam, or did we merely play out an institutional repertoire devised for fighting Soviet and Warsaw Pact forces in Europe?

In the years since 1973, the Air Force has returned to its focus on nuclear and conventional scenarios for a war in Europe. Battles for the budget and a preoccupation with acquiring newer, more sophisticated planes and weapons occupy many of the Air Force's finest officers, enforcing the bureaucratic rather than the warrior ethic. With its eyes fixed simultaneously on grand strategic warfare against enemies with similar industrial and military institutions and on the "Planning, Programming and Budgeting System," the Air Force has tended to ignore the lessons of Vietnam, just as it did the lessons that should have been learned from Korea. Given that most experts believe that future wars will more closely resemble the one we lost in Southeast Asia rather than the one we won in 1945, this attitude could have grave consequences. Fifty-seven thousand Americans, including over 2,000 airmen, gave their lives for something better than that.

NOTES

1. Carl Berger, editor, *The United States Air Force in Southeast Asia, 1961–1973: An Illustrated Account*, 1984 revised edition (Washington, D.C.: Office of Air Force History), p. 369.

2. Major Suzanne Budd Gehri, *Study War Once More: Teaching Vietnam at Air University* (Maxwell Air Force Base, Ala.: Center for Aerospace Doctrine, Research, and Education, 1985), p. 6.

3. Colonel Thomas A. Fabyanic, "War, Doctrine, and the Air War College," *Air University Review*, January-February 1986, pp. 15–18.

4. For a more or less typical senior officer's perspective on air power in Vietnam, see the conclusion of General William W. Momyer, *Air Power in Three Wars* (Washington, D.C.: U.S. Government Printing Office, 1977), pp. 337–40.

5. Colonel Harry G. Summers, Jr., *On Strategy: A Critical Analysis of the Vietnam War* (Novato, Calf.: Presidio Press, 1982), p. 1.

6. General William C. Westmoreland, *A Soldier Reports* (Garden City, New York: Doubleday and Company, Inc., 1976), p. 234.

7. Dave Richard Palmer, *Summons of the Trumpet: U.S.–Vietnam in Perspective* (San Rafael, Cal.: Presidio Press, 1978), pp. 107–15.

8. Sun Tzu, *The Art of War*, Samuel B. Griffith, editor (reprint; London: Oxford University Press, 1977), p. 73.

9. George C. Marshall, quoted in Russell Weigley, *The American Way of War* (New York: Macmillan Publishing Company, Inc., 1973), p. 5.

10. Edward Doyle and Samuel Lipsman, editors, *The Vietnam Experience*, vol. 4, *American Takes Over* (Boston, Mass.: Boston Publishing Company, 1982), p. 70. The discussion of North Vietnamese strategy indicates that the North Vietnamese decided America would quit the war when 50,000 American troops had been killed.

11. Thomas C. Thayer, *War Without Fronts: The American Experience in Vietnam* (Boulder, Colo.: Westview Press, 1985), pp. 17–18.

12. Westmoreland, *A Soldier*, p. 337.

13. Momyer, *Air Power*, p. 213.

14. Lieutenant Colonel Henry Zeybel, "Truck Count," *Air University Review* (January-February 1983), p. 45.

15. Henry A. Kissinger, *The White House Years* (New York: Little, Brown and Company, 1979), p. 241.

16. Palmer, *Summons of the Trumpet*, pp. 233–40.

17. Raphael Littauer and Norman Uphoff, eds., *The Air War in Indochina* (Boston, Mass.: Beacon Press, 1971), pp. 198–201.

18. Guenter Lewy, *America in Vietnam* (New York: Oxford University Press, 1978), pp. 406–407. Professor Lewy makes the point that "protective reaction strikes" against

SAM sites soon expanded to "limited duration protective reaction strikes," which, in 1970, included 1,113 attack sorties flown against supply dumps, staging areas, and other targets that were not specifically related to SAM or antiaircraft sites. This provided the backdrop for the secret bombing of North Vietnam carried out by the Seventh Air Force Commander, General John D. Lavalle, between November 1971 and March 1972. When the subterfuges involved in these bombings were revealed, the credibility of the government and the Air Force suffered accordingly.

19. Lieutenant Colonel Monte D. Wright, *USAF Tactics Against Air and Ground Defenses in SEA, November 1968–May 1970* (Hq PACAF: Project CHECO, 25 September 1970), p. 1; and USFA Management Summary for Southeast Asia (24 September 1969), p. 38.

20. Interview with Major William A. Buckingham, Jr., Office of Air Force History, Washington, D.C., 20 April 1979. Major Buckingham related a story told to him by a former targeteer in the American embassy in Phnom Penh. According to the targeteer, after Neak Luong, a Cambodian naval base, was accidentally bombed by B–52s, he started submitting fictitious "underwater storage areas" as targets because the Air Force insisted on flying a certain number of B–52 sorties into Cambodia everyday, regardless of whether there were targets suitable for a B–52 strike. In an interview, on 1 May 1980, Major Buckingham and the author asked former Ambassador to Cambodia Colby Swank if there was any truth to this allegation. While the ambassador did not confirm the targeteer's remarks, he said these allegations had "an element of truth" to them "in that [General John Vogt] had these sorties to be used."

21. "Igloo White," *Air Force Magazine* (June 1971), p. 48.

22. Cecil B. Currey, *Self-Destruction: The Disintegration and Decay of the United States Army During the Vietnam Era* (New York: W. W. Norton and Company, 1981), pp. 143–45. For an excellent example of the "can do" attitude in the Air Force, see the film *There Is A Way*, Air Force Now Series, 1352d Photo Group, Robert F. Engle, producer.

23. See, Major John Schlight, *Rescue at Ban Phanop*, 5–7 December 1969 (Hq PACAF: Project CHECO, 1970), pp. 12–13; and Major Earl H. Tilford, Jr., *The United States Air Force Search and Rescue in Southeast Asia, 1961–75* (Washington, D.C.: Office of Air Force History, 1980), p. 119.

24. See, A.J.C. Lavalle, editor, *Airpower and the Spring Invasion* (Washington, D.C.: U.S. Government Printing Office, 1976), pp. 36–41; and Tilford, pp. 118–19.

25. See, Wallace J. Thies, *When Governments Collide: Operations and Diplomacy in the Vietnam Conflict, 1964–1968* (Berkley, Cal.: University of California, 1980), pp. 82–94; James Clay Thompson, *Rolling Thunder: Understanding Policy and Program Failure* (Chapel Hill: University of North Carolina Press, 1980), pp. 27–34; and memorandum, McGeorge Bundy to President Johnson, "Sustained Reprisal Policy," (7 February 1965), cited in *Pentagon Papers*, pp. 433–435.

26. W. Hays Parks, "Rolling Thunder and the Law of War," *Air University Review*, January-February 1982, p. 13.

27. See, Doris Kearns, *Lyndon Johnson and the American Dream* (New York: Harper and Row, 1976), pp. 264–65. Kearns relates Johnson's fears that a misplaced bomb might have brought on Chinese or Soviet intervention. According to Kearns, Johnson thought the bombing should be "seduction and not rape." In other words, Johnson wanted to use the bombing to pressure the North Vietnamese politically.

28. Thayer, *War Without Fronts*, p. 79. See, also, Frances FitzGerald, *Fire in the*

Lake: The Vietnamese and Americans in Vietnam (New York: Little, Brown, 1971), and Joseph Buttinger, *The Smaller Dragon: A Political History of Vietnam* (New York: Praeger, 1958). Together, these two books give an excellent view of Vietnamese culture and society.

29. See, Lieutenant Colonel Stanley J. Michael, Jr., "Vietnam: Failure to Follow the Principles of War," *Marine Corps Gazette* (August 1977), pp. 57–62; and Palmer, *Summons of the Trumpet*, pp. 72–80.

30. Lewy, *America in Vietnam*, p. 390.

31. Ibid., p. 391.

32. Tilford, *Search and Rescue*, p. 121.

33. Lewy, *America in Vietnam*, p. 391.

34. Ibid., p. 410.

35. Stanley Karnow, *Vietnam: A History* (New York: Viking Press, 1983), pp. 652–653.

36. See: George C. Herring, *America's Longest War: The United States in Vietnam, 1950–1975* (New York: Random House, 1979), p. 248; and Loren Baritz, *Backfire* (New York: Ballatine Books, 1985), p. 215.

37. See: General T.R. Milton, USAF (Ret.), "The Lessons of Vietnam," *Air Force Magazine* (March 1983), p. 109. Writing in the January-February 1983 issue of *Air University Review*, p. 53, Lt. Col. John F. Piowaty, in "Reflections of a Thud Driver," expressed a similar viewpoint, "By the time President Nixon got serious and won in two weeks (referencing *Linebacker II*) what we could have done in any two weeks for nearly a decade, it was too late to hold the victory."

IV

WERE THERE ALTERNATIVE STRATEGIES?

Given contradictory perceptions about the war's nature and the lack of clear U.S. objectives, advice on strategy followed suit: contradictory and conflicting strategy prescriptions became routine. Moreover, the United States confused strategy with tactics. The best articulated strategy confrontation was between the conventional war strategists and the unconventional war—counterinsurgency advocates. Their differences were fundamental: The first focused on the threat from the North and wanted to smash North Vietnamese units operating against the South. The second focused on the internal problems of South Vietnam, advocating a strong ARVN defense effort, a population protection strategy, and a political-economic reform.

The debate over alternative strategies began before U.S. regular units entered combat in 1965. As Colonel Harry Summers points out in his essay "A Strategic Perception of the Vietnam War," early British and American advisors to the Diem government saw the problems in South Vietnam as fundamentally political and advocated measures similar to those used in Malaya. However, once regular NVA units appeared in South Vietnam, the U.S. military response became almost wholly conventional. Still, in Colonel Summers's view, that response was misplaced because it missed the heart of the problem—North Vietnam's ability to wage war.

Nevertheless, for all the "other war" rhetoric, in terms of *resources*, counterinsurgency and revolutionary warfare were never given serious attention. Robert Komer's vigorous integration of U.S. pacification *advisory* efforts in the late 1960s focused some U.S. (and GVN) attention on the problem, but the U.S. pacification advisory effort never got more than 10 percent of the U.S. resources spent in South Vietnam.

As the main-force war intensified, and the grim human damage mounted in South Vietnam—with more than twice as many civilians dying as soldiers—proposals kept surfacing to reorient U.S. strategy toward population protection and territorial security. A more balanced mix of attrition and population protection would have helped because evidence accumulated that the Communists were attacking the South Vietnamese population—fighting a dispersed, small unit war designed to keep the population insecure while distracting and wearing down U.S./GVN forces. With a vast majority of NVA/VC attacks at below battalion level, the unconventional nature of the communist attack became apparent.

In analyzing Communist strategy and the US/GVN response, Colonel Peter Dunn and Dr. Noel Eggleston argue that it was the communists' attack on the South Vietnamese population (the RVN's "center of gravity") and US public opinion that most reflected their strategy. What Colonel Summers calls a "smoke screen," Colonel Dunn argues was, in reality, *the* means to victory: "They attacked American strategy, building political alliances that outflanked Washington and devising tactics to negate search and destroy tactics." Rather than using Clausewitz, the Vietnamese Communists relied on *Asian* revolutionary war strategists, particularly Sun Tzu and Mao Zedong and, of course, Vo Nguyen Giap. By attacking the strategy of the United States and Saigon, Colonel Dunn believes that the Vietnamese Communists clearly understood the psychological and political elements of strategy. Dr. Eggleston, in examining Colonel Summers's alternative strategy ideas—attacking the North earlier in the war and that North Vietnam could have been made to surrender—believes Summers misread history and underestimated not only the Communists' ability to absorb punishment but also, as compared to the United States, their staying power. "Ultimately," he asks, "who cared more about the fate of South Vietnam—the Viet Cong and the North Vietnamese or the United States?" Finally, in clearly contrasting his views to Colonel Summers's views, Colonel Dunn gives us his bottom line: "Had Clausewitz been alive in our time and serving as an American general officer, he too probably would have lost this war. His theory demands a target, an enemy army to destroy; and the Communists would not have offered him such a target."

6

Harry G. Summers, Jr.

A Strategic Perception of the Vietnam War

There is a famous Jules Feiffer cartoon in which one of the characters, having just made what he believes to be the telling point of a long and involved argument, is devastated by the riposte "Now let us define your terms." To avoid such a fate, it is best to define your terms in advance, and for this particular argument the main term to be defined is *strategic*, for there is a fundamental difference between strategic perceptions of the Vietnam War and historical perceptions of that conflict.

Military strategy is officially defined as "the art and science of employing the armed forces of a nation to secure the objectives of national policy by the application of force, or the threat of force."[1] Strategic appraisal of the Vietnam War, therefore, would properly involve an examination of that war through the application of theoretical principles to both the military means employed and the political ends that were to be achieved, not only to account for success or failure but also to revalidate the principles themselves. Karl von Clausewitz, that master theoretician on the nature and conduct of war, labeled this process "critical analysis," a procedure that involves three different intellectual activities.

The first of these is "the discovery and interpretation of equivocal facts . . . historical research proper." Then there is "the tracing of effects back to their causes." Up to this point, historical and strategic analysis travel the same path, for most military historians would agree that these first two intellectual activities accurately describe the nature of their profession. But with the next intellectual activity the paths diverge. The third process is "the investigation and evaluation of means employed," and Clausewitz went on to say that "critical analysis is not only an evaluation of the means employed, but of *all possible means* . . .

Reprinted with the permission of Colonel Summers and *Parameters*. Originally published in *Parameters*, June 1983, Volume XIII, No. 2, pp. 41–46.

One can, after all, not condemn a method without being able to suggest a better alternative."[2]

What this divergence of paths tells us is that while the test of a work of military history is the degree to which it accurately portrays precisely what happened and why, military theory is tested "by the application of theoretical truths to actual events." "Here," Clausewitz said, "theory serves history, or rather the lessons to be drawn from history."[3] Simply put, military history provides us with a set of answers. Military theory, on the other hand, provides what our current doctrinal manuals describe as "military planning interrogatories—a set of questions that should be considered if military strategy is to best serve the national interest."[4]

THE FIRST STRATEGIC QUESTION

In *On War* Clausewitz emphasized that

the first, the supreme, the most far-reaching act of judgment that the statesman and commander have to make is to establish . . . the kind of war on which they are embarking; neither mistaking it for, nor trying to turn it into, something that is alien to its nature. This is the first of all strategic questions and the most comprehensive.[5]

Practically from the beginning of our involvement in Vietnam, the received "theoretical truth" was that the conflict there was a *revolutionary* war. Sir Robert Thompson, British expert on insurgent warfare, explained how revolutionary war differed from conventional:

Revolutionary war is most confused with guerrilla or partisan warfare. Here the main difference is that guerrilla warfare is designed merely to harass and distract the enemy so that the regular forces can reach a decision in conventional battles. . . . Revolutionary war on the other hand is designed to reach a decisive result on its own.[6]

With this "new kind of war," conventional military histories were deemed useless, and the classic theories and principles of war derived from these histories by Clausewitz, Jomini, Liddell Hart, J. F. C. Fuller, and others were considered irrelevant. They had been replaced by the works of Mao Tse-tung and Vo Nguyen Giap on revolutionary war and the theories of academic "counterinsurgency experts."

The model for such a war was not derived from our then-recent experience in Korea where we also had fought to contain communist expansion, but from the British experience in Malaysia. As British researcher Gregory Palmer noted:

The official view supported by the advice of Diem's British Advisor, Sir Robert Thompson, was that the appropriate strategy was counterinsurgency with emphasis on depriving the enemy of the support of the population by resettlement, pacification, good administration, and propaganda.[7]

Counterinsurgency doctrines thus channeled our attention toward the internal affairs of the South Vietnamese government rather than toward the external threat.

Clausewitz observed that "we see things in the light of their result, and to some extent, come to know and appreciate them fully only because of it."[8] If we apply the theoretical truths of revolutionary war to the actual events of the Vietnam War, we find that they do not fit. The Viet Cong did not achieve decisive results on their own. Instead, their actions fit Sir Robert Thompson's description of "guerrilla or partisan warfare" almost exactly—they harassed, distracted, and wore down the United States and South Vietnam so that by 1975 the regular forces of North Vietnam could reach a decision in conventional battles. In the Afterword to a collection of papers presented at a 1973–74 colloquium on "the Military Lessons of the Vietnam War" at the Fletcher School of Law and Diplomacy, where more than 30 distinguished military and civilian panelists discussed the merits of counterinsurgency, panel organizers Air Force Colonel Donald D. Frizzell and Professor W. Scott Thompson sadly concluded:

There is great irony in the fact that the North Vietnamese finally won by purely conventional means, using precisely the kind of warfare at which the American army was best equipped to fight . . . In their lengthy battle accounts that followed Hanoi's great military victory, Generals Giap and Dung barely mentioned the contribution of local forces.[9]

Only in retrospect is it obvious that the North Vietnamese used the smoke screen of revolutionary war to hide their true intentions. Part of this smoke screen was the so-called National Liberation Front, which was portrayed as an indigenous South Vietnamese organization leading the revolutionary war against the Saigon regime. With victory long since won, the North Vietnamese have not bothered to keep up this pretense and now freely admit that the NLF was their own creation. In a French television documentary broadcast on February 16, 1983, North Vietnamese Generals Vo Nguyen Giap and Vo Bam freely admitted their subterfuge. As reported by *The Economist*:

General Bam admitted the decision to unleash an armed revolt against the Saigon government was taken by a North Vietnamese communist party plenum in 1959. This was a year before the National Liberation Front was set up in South Vietnam. The aim, General Bam added, was "to reunite the country." So much for that myth that the Vietcong was an autonomous southern force which spontaneously decided to rise against the oppression of the Diem regime. And General Bam should know. As a result of the decision, he was given the job of opening up an infiltration trail in the south. The year was still 1959. That was two years before President Kennedy stepped up American support for Diem by sending 685 advisers to South Vietnam. So much for the story that the Ho Chi Minh trail was established only to counteract the American military build-up. . . . General Bam got his orders on May 19, 1959. "Absolute secrecy, absolute security were our watchwords," he recalled.[10]

It is not surprising that we were deceived, for many South Vietnamese members of the NLF were equally deluded. But now the denouements of former NLF leaders such as Truong Nhu Tang[11] provide valuable sources for "the discovery and interpretation of equivocal facts [and] the tracings of effects back to their causes." With such a reexamination it will become increasingly apparent that, unlike the First Indochina War between France and the Vietminh, which *was* a revolutionary war, the Second Indochina War between North Vietnam and South Vietnam was, in the final analysis, a more conventional war best understood in terms of classic military theories and principles. Among these are the principles of the *Objective,* and of *Mass, Maneuver*, and *Economy of Force.*[12]

THE OBJECTIVE

"No one starts a war," wrote Clausewitz, "or rather, no one in his senses ought to do so—without first being clear in his mind what he intends to achieve by that war and how he intends to conduct it."[13] Since 1921 this warning has been incorporated into the Army's doctrine as the first Principle of War—the principle of the Objective.[14] In the words of the current Army doctrinal manual:

As a derivative of the political aim, the *strategic military objective* of a nation at war must be to apply whatever degree of force is necessary to allow attainment of the political purpose or aim for which the war is being fought. . . . It is essential . . . that the political purpose be clearly defined *and* attainable by the considered application of the various elements of the nation's power. Not until the political purpose has been determined and defined by the President and the Congress can strategic and tactical objectives be clearly identified and developed. Once developed, the strategic objectives must constantly be subjected to rigorous analysis and review to insure that they continue to reflect accurately not only the ultimate political end desired, but also any political constraints imposed on the application of military force.[15]

As with our failure to determine accurately the nature of the war in Vietnam, the application of this strategic principle seems never to have been one marked by precision and consistency—as the actual events of American participation amply illustrate. Examining the *official* justifications most often cited from 1949 through 1967 for America's involvement in Indochina, Professor Hugh M. Arnold found that, compared to the *one* North Vietnamese objective of total control over all of Indochina, there were some 22 separate American rationales.[16] None of them focused on how the war was to be ended. When Secretary of Defense Clark Clifford took office in 1968, he complained that no one in the Defense Department could tell him what constituted victory. No one could tell him of a plan to win the war.[17] This confusion over objectives had a devastating effect on our ability to conduct the war. As Brigadier General Douglas Kinnard found in a 1974 survey of Army generals who had commanded in Vietnam, "Almost 70 percent of the Army generals who managed the war were uncertain of its objectives." Kinnard went on to say that such uncertainty "mirrors a deep-seated strategic failure: the inability of policy-makers to frame tangible, obtainable goals.[18]

Vietnam-era military theorists not only failed to set objectives, they also deliberately excluded the American public from the strategic equation. Theorists went so far as to say that military strategies ought to be pursued even when they are opposed by the American people.[19] This approach not only violated our American political and military heritage and both the intent and letter of the Constitution, it also violated a fundamental precept of war. Modern warfare, Clausewitz emphasized, consists of "a remarkable trinity" of the people, the army, and the government. "A theory that ignores any one of them . . . would conflict with reality to such an extent that for this reason alone it would be totally useless."[20] As he would have predicted, the effect of the deliberate exclusion of the American people as a prime consideration in strategic planning was deadly. In the Vietnam War, unlike previous American conflicts, the American people were being asked to bear the cost of a war whose "value" had neither been fixed nor adequately justified by their government. One hundred fifty years earlier Clausewitz had warned: "Since war is not an act of senseless passion but is controlled by its political object, the value of this object must determine the sacrifices to be made for it in *magnitude* and also in *duration*."[21] In words that seem to have been written to explain Vietnam, he went on to say, "Once the expenditure of effort exceeds the value of the political object, the object must be renounced."[22] Our failure to understand and apply the principle of the objective and the other fundamentals of war created a strategic vulnerability that was to prove fatal to American war efforts.

MASS, MANEUVER, AND ECONOMY OF FORCE

Faulty strategic thinking, not surprisingly, led to faulty military operations in the field. The primary principles that govern battlefield operations are *Mass* (the concentration of combat power at the decisive place and time), *Economy of Force* (the allocation of minimum essential combat power to secondary efforts), and *Maneuver* (the placing of the enemy in a position of disadvantage through the flexible application of combat power).[23] In theory, these three principles operate in concert against what Clausewitz called the enemy's center of gravity— "the hub of all power and movement on which everything depends." The center of gravity can be tangible, such as the enemy's army, its territory, or its capital, but it also can be something abstract, such as the community of interests of an alliance, the personality of a leader, or public opinion. Once identified, the center of gravity becomes the focal point against which all military energies should be directed.[24]

Because we failed to correctly identify the nature of the war, we also failed to identify the center of gravity for that war. Because we misperceived the Vietnam War as a revolutionary war, we saw the Viet Cong as the center of gravity. Our efforts were massed against this guerrilla enemy in search-and-destroy and pacification efforts, while we used an economy of force against the North Vietnamese regular forces. Contrary to popular opinion, these efforts against the Viet Cong had considerable military success. This was especially true during the Tet Offensive of 1968 in which the Viet Cong guerrillas surfaced, led the attacks on South Vietnamese cities, and were virtually destroyed in the process. Former NLF member Truong Nhu Tang called it "a military debacle." "The truth was," he said, "that Tet cost us half of our forces. Our losses were so immense that we were simply unable to replace them with new recruits."[25] But even after the Viet Cong were virtually eliminated, the war continued unabated for another seven years.

We had selected the wrong center of gravity. The key was not the Viet Cong nor the allegiance of the South Vietnamese people. "Like us, Hanoi failed to win the 'hearts and minds' of the South Vietnamese peasantry," Colonel Stuart Herrington wrote in his account of counterinsurgency operations. "Unlike us, Hanoi's leaders were able to compensate for this failure by playing their trump card—they overwhelmed South Vietnam with a twenty-two division force."[26] The results of the war clearly demonstrate that the primary enemy was the North Vietnamese regular army; the Viet Cong were never more than a secondary force. As Norman Hannah, the former State Department political advisor to the Commander-in-Chief, Pacific Command (the war's strategic commander), put it, "We responded mainly to Hanoi's simulated insurgency rather than to its real, but controlled aggression, as a bull charges the toreador's cape, not the toreador."[27] Our concentration on a secondary enemy frittered away our military resources on inconclusive military and social operations that ultimately exhausted the patience of the American people. Because we did not properly define our terms at the outset, we ended up defeating ourselves.

CONCLUSION

Through Clausewitzian "critical analysis"—i.e., by testing classic military theory against the actual events of the Vietnam War—one is left with a strategic perception of the Vietnam War that reveals, among other things, that much of the existing historical perception is faulty. This is not surprising, for scholars have always rightly been suspicious of works written in the heat of passion, which too often mirror the prejudices of the times.

But, ten years after the American withdrawal from Vietnam, passions are beginning to cool. In his examination of "The New Vietnam Scholarship," Asian scholar and former Vietnam War correspondent Fox Butterfield called attention to

the emergence of a small group of scholars, journalists and military specialists who have started to look afresh at the war. . . . For most of these scholars, their re-examination is not to prove whether Vietnam was or was not a 'noble cause,' in President Reagan's phrase, but to find out what really happened and why.[28]

As noted earlier, military historians and military strategists share a common interest in finding out "what really happened and why." To this end, the study of the military history of not only the Vietnam War but all past wars has been reintroduced into the entire Army educational system. But the study of military history is not an end in itself, only a means to the further end of "providing a thinking man with a frame of reference." If it is to accomplish this task, military history must be subjected to what Clausewitz called an "analytical investigation leading to a close acquaintance with the subject." As he said, "It is precisely that inquiry which is the most essential part of any *theory*." And it is only after such inquiry, he said, that theory "becomes a guide to anyone who wants to learn about war from books; it will light his way, ease his progress, train his judgment, and help him to avoid pitfalls."[29]

Strategic analysis of the war in Vietnam cannot change the tragic results of our involvement there. But if it can train our judgment and help us avoid such pitfalls in the future, our experience there will not have been totally in vain.

NOTES

1. *JCS Pub. 1: Dictionary of Military and Associated Terms* (Washington, D.C.: The Joint Chiefs of Staff, 1979), p. 217.

2. Karl von Clausewitz, *On War*, ed. and trans. by Michael Howard and Peter Paret, with introductory essays by Peter Paret, Michael Howard, and Bernard Brodie, and a commentary by Bernard Brodie (Princeton, N.J.: Princeton University Press, 1976), pp. 156, 161.

3. Ibid.

4. U.S. Department of the Army, *The Army*, Field Manual 100–1 (Washington, D.C.: GPO, 1981), p. 13.

5. Clausewitz, *War*, pp. 88–89.

6. Sir Robert Thompson, *Revolutionary War in World Strategy, 1945–1969* (New York: Taplinger Publishing Co., 1970), pp. 16–17.

7. Gregory Palmer, *The McNamara Strategy and the Vietnam War: Program Budgeting in the Pentagon, 1960–1968* (Westport, Conn.: Greenwood Press, 1978), pp. 99–100.

8. Clausewitz, *War*, p. 165.

9. W. Scott Thompson and Donald D. Frizzell, ed., *The Lessons of Vietnam* (New York: Crane, Russak & Co., 1977), p. 279.

10. "Vietnam: We Lied to You," *The Economist*, 26 February 1983, pp. 56–57.

11. Truong Nhu Tang, "The Myth of a Liberation," *New York Review of Books*, 21 October 1982, pp. 31–36.

12. For a complete critical analysis of the Vietnam War based on the principles of war, see my *On Strategy: A Critical Analysis of the Vietnam War* (Novato, Cal.: Presidio Press, 1982), chaps. 9–14.

13. Clausewitz, *War*, p. 579.

14. For a detailed analysis of the Principles of War, see John I. Alger, *The Quest for Victory* (Westport, Conn.: Greenwood Press, 1982).

15. Army, Field Manual 100–1, p. 14.

16. Hugh M. Arnold, "Official Justifications for America's Role in Indochina, 1949–67," *Asian Affairs*, 3 (September–October 1975), 31.

17. Michael MacLear, *The Ten Thousand Day War, Vietnam: 1945–1975* (New York: St. Martin's Press, 1981), p. 216.

18. Douglas Kinnard, *The War Managers* (Hanover, N.H.: Univ. Press of New England, 1977), p. 25.

19. Stephen Peter Rosen, "Vietnam and the American Theory of Limited War," *International Security* 7 (Fall 1982), 85.

20. Clausewitz, *War*, p. 89.

21. Ibid., p. 92.

22. Ibid.

23. Army, Field Manual 100–1, pp. 14–15.

24. Clausewitz, *War*, pp. 595–97.

25. Tang, *Liberations*, p. 32.

26. Stuart A. Herrington, *Silence Was a Weapon: The Vietnam War in the Villages* (Novato, Cal.: Presidio Press, 1982), p. 203.

27. Norman B. Hannah, "Vietnam: Now We Know," in *All Quiet on the Eastern Front*, ed. Anthony T. Bouscaren (New York: Devin-Adair, 1977), p. 149.

28. Fox Butterfield, "The New Vietnam Scholarship: Challenging the Old Passions," *The New York Times Magazine*, 13 February 1983, pp. 26–28.

29. Clausewitz, *War*, p. 141.

On Strategy Revisited: Clausewitz and Revolutionary War

Colonel Harry G. Summers's critical analysis of American strategy (or lack of it) during the Vietnam War was a timely and desperately needed examination of the United States' first clear defeat in war. He has done what no governmental institution has been able to bring itself to do. There are absolutely vital lessons to be learned from *On Strategy: A Critical Analysis of the Vietnam War*.

Colonel Summers's thesis may be roughly summed up as follows: It is by using as a yardstick the theories of the Prussian General Karl von Clausewitz, whose life spanned the eighteenth and nineteenth centuries, that the conduct of the United States in the Vietnam War can be measured and progress evaluated. Certain inhibiting factors—called *friction* by Clausewitz for want of a better word—in the American culture impeded the efficient prosecution of the war. These included the people, their elected political representatives, potentially unacceptable political and military risks, and faulty military doctrines and beliefs. In addition, an incorrect assessment of the true nature of the war, coupled with a departure from certain general principles of war, contributed to the American failure. Ultimately, all of these ills evolved from the shallowness of the top political and military leaders in the United States.

More specifically, the analysis in *On Strategy* is divided into two parts: "The Environment" and the conduct of the war, "The Engagement." The following theses are manifested in the Environment section: U.S. military leaders failed to emphasize the horrors of war to their civilian leaders; the Army should not have been committed to a long war without arousing the American people; and American leaders chose to avoid mobilizing the people in order to avoid a nuclear war with the large socialist countries (the Soviet Union and China). Colonel Summers sees the Korean Conflict—where the United Nations forces were smashed on the Yalu River and thrown back to the South Korean border—as a precedent in what is now called "limited war."[1] He also recognizes the brittleness of American society—if Americans do not win their wars in a weekend, they tire of them. Three decades ago, General Vo Nguyen Giap recognized this problem in the Western democracies when he said:

The enemy will pass slowly from the offensive to the defensive. The blitzkrieg will transform itself into a war of long duration. Thus, the enemy will be caught in a dilemma: he has to drag out the war in order to win it and does not possess, on the other hand, the psychological and political means to fight a long drawn-out war.[2]

Note that General Giap emphasized the psychological and political means to fight, rather than military means. And while these words were written of the French imperialists, they applied equally to what the communists called the American neocolonialists.

The American answer, as some saw it, was to consider declaring war on North Vietnam in order to focus the attention of the American people on the war against the communists. However, the implications of this action were apparent even to the "hawks" in the government. By losing sight of their purpose, civilian and military leaders squandered their energies in uncoordinated efforts at containing communists.

There is acknowledgment in *On Strategy* that the unfair application of conscription contributed to the problems—the more affluent were rewarded by avoiding the war, while the less fortunate people (the poor and the unrepresented) were drafted and sent to the front.

It seems unbelievable that the political leaders and senior generals spoke so little to each other; most of the strategy seems to have been devised by civilians with political connections to the ruling party. Fortunately for the communists, as Colonel Summers points out, this strategy allowed the North Vietnamese to wage war in the south while no American or South Vietnamese troops were allowed to invade any part of the north. (Even after the Paris Accords, the United States, over furious Saigon protests, was generous enough to let communist forces remain in the south *after* the American retreat.)

U.S. officials later admitted (as North Vietnam had earlier recognized) their fear of the People's Republic of China and, to a certain extent, the Soviet Union. Abhorrence of nuclear war severely limited the American strategy in Indochina. While North Vietnam played to its strengths by fighting a people's war, some Americans debunked the communist strategy (and people's war) as propaganda. They saw only regular forces (although, in part, this assessment may have been the product of wishful thinking.) Americans were limited by their own doctrines, such as they were, and the quality of their senior leaders (who had little time to think). They thought that because North Vietnam had some units of the People's Liberation Armed Forces in South Vietnam, the war was a "regular" war (as the U.S. Armed Forces understood it), to be fought by regular soldiers using regular tactics. They cite as proof of this the final communist campaign to achieve the Great Spring Victory in 1975. (Thus Americans once again, according to the North Vietnamese, showed their failure to understand modern war.) Further, military officers claim that the U.S. military forces were asked to perform other than purely military tasks, and these functions were a burden to the Army.

This complaint is somewhat puzzling, for Clausewitz emphasized the political nature of war, which means that violence is only a portion of the overall political process. If an army knows only how to dispense violence, it leaves to others—civilians—the tasks of performing other essential functions in the social and economic spheres. Paradoxically, the fact that so many civilians become involved in the planning and execution of American wars is a major U.S. military complaint.

But by Clausewitz's own thinking, the American response to communist actions in the south was probably correct. Limited aims call for limited measures. Had the Americans widened the war, as some now insist should have been done, the means would have been out of proportion to the ends; and if these expanded means had brought an expanded war with more active involvement by North Vietnam's Chinese and Soviet allies, the United States would have turned Clausewitz on his head.

THE NATURE OF THE WAR IN VIETNAM

The second part of *On Strategy*, titled ''The Engagement,'' deals with strategic and operational matters, including what appear to be a fairly rigid handling of the ''principles of war.'' However, before we can discuss America's Vietnam War within the context of Summers's book, it must be recognized that the war—both during its prosecution and after its end—meant different things to different people. Some thought it a revolutionary war; others, a conventional war. Some called it an American defeat; others, a draw. Some say that it could have been won; others dispute that contention. Some say that U.S. forces won all their battles, while others refute that claim. On few other such subjects are feelings so deep or opinions so divided.

Thus, the fundamental question to be resolved in any discussion of the American war in Vietnam is this: What sort of war was it? Colonel Summers states clearly that it was a straightforward, conventional war and that Vietnamese Communist writers and leaders are not to be believed when they describe the war as a revolutionary war. Yet all the North Vietnamese, including Senior Generals Vo Nguyen Giap and Van Tien Dung, have stated unequivocally *that the war they directed was a revolutionary war*. And since General Dung wrote after the Democratic Republic of Vietnam (DRV) had won total victory over South Vietnam,[3] we can assume that there would now be no apparent reason for him, or other DRV officials, to somehow mask the true nature of the war as they prosecuted it. For the victors, at least, it was a revolutionary war.

Colonel Summers and some others deny that there was any significant aspect of civil war in the struggle between the northern and southern halves of Vietnam. But what makes this war so different from an earlier war between northern and southern province over the latter's right to have its own sovereign state—from the American Civil War? South Vietnam was as artificial a creation as the Confederate States of America, and the Union's conquest and reunification with the southern states was in many ways a tactical blueprint for North Vietnam's conquest of the south and the reunification of Vietnam.

Next, we must ask whether there is only one form or one stereotype of revolutionary war, or are there mutations to fit different environments and political climates? If one thinks that there is but a single stereotype, then one may also think like Raymond Aron, who stated that because the armed forces that captured Saigon in 1975 did not spring from the southern guerrillas, the war could not be called a revolutionary war.[4]

But the communists themselves put no such straitjacket on their concept of revolutionary war which, according to Mao is flexible and, like water, fits the environment.[5] For one thing, the Vietnamese Communists made no distinction between the people of the North and South. It is important here to depart from the conventional Western approach to Vietnam. Whether true or not, the communists saw themselves as morally and psychologically superior to the south, whose people awaited liberation from the quisling Saigon apparatus and their neocolonialist (American) masters.

CLAUSEWITZ: WAS HE REALLY RELEVANT TO VIETNAM?

Can we look to Clausewitz for the reasons for the American failure in Indochina, or are there other masters of war who would be more appropriate in this context? A reading of *On War* suggests that it may be unrealistic to look only to Clausewitz for the reasons for failure in Vietnam. Clausewitz was to war and politics what Newton and Galileo were to physics and astronomy: what they did became universal laws, but their fields have expanded immeasurably beyond their works.

Clausewitz knew nothing of mass political movements, revolutionary war, or urban guerrilla warfare—the dominant features of contemporary world conflicts. Thus, although we might like to use his works as our universal authority, we cannot turn to him for any ideas on how to address these seemingly intractable problems. In fact, even modern "regular" warfare may have rendered questionable some of the principles of Clausewitz. For example, how would he deal with the principle of massed attack in this age of tactical nuclear weapons, including artillery?

It is often overlooked that Clausewitz himself cautioned his readers not to take his work as gospel; indeed, he intended to rethink and rewrite much of his work, but he died before he could do so. As Basil Liddell Hart noted:

The ill-effects of Clausewitz's teachings arose largely from his disciples' too shallow and too extreme interpretation of it, overlooking his qualifying clauses, but he lent himself to such misinterpretation by expounding his theory in a way too abstract and involved for concrete-minded soldiers to follow the course of his argument, which often turned back from the direction which it seemed to be taking.[6]

Thus Clausewitz, in some ways, was like the Vietnam War itself; he, like it, was many things to many people. It has been written that this war was like the elephant to the six blind men: all thought that they recognized parts of it, but none was able to comprehend the whole.[7]

Given how much is placed on the shoulders of Clausewitz by our military officers concerned with strategy, it is interesting to note that the first American translation of *On War* did not appear until World War II (1943), 34 years after the previously published English edition. Moreover, for most of the century after his death, German authorities frequently altered the words of Clausewitz to suit their own interests.

Clausewitz drew his theories largely from studying the campaigns of Frederick the Great and Napoleon. The opposing forces were easily distinguishable and ponderous in movement. The populations were not organized to the smallest village and city block, so that decisions taken at the national level may or may not have filtered down to the smallest unit of communal life. Certainly the nation was unable to respond like modern organized Marxist states. Napoleonic armies were unable to split up rapidly and disperse into the countryside or to regroup equally rapidly at will and switch from light mobile warfare to conventional heavy warfare. The wars studied by Clausewitz occurred on the same continent, almost always between neighboring states, and in terrain suited for the movement of large armies. How would the difficult roadless karst and mountainous jungle country as found in Asia have influenced him?

For us, the most pertinent of Napoleon's campaigns drew only passing reference by Clausewitz, who wrote: "The stubborn resistance of the Spaniards, marred as it was by weakness and inadequacy of particulars, showed what can be accomplished by arming a people and by insurrection."[8] The very word *guerrilla* came from his campaign, but it escaped Clausewitz's serious attention, for he was focused on a different kind of war (in many ways, an easier kind of war). Yet the "little war" in Spain bled the French to the bone, and despite the unspeakable cruelties inflicted on the Spanish people, the French—harried also by a small British expeditionary force—had to withdraw. Clausewitz's theories would be truly complete had he devoted more time to the "little war," for it was this type of war that enabled a relatively weak nation, North Vietnam, to defeat the United States.

SUN TZU: REVOLUTIONARY WAR IN THE ASIAN CONTEXT

If we must look to someone to find the fundamental reasons for America's lack of success in Vietnam, perhaps we should reexamine the ancient (yet startlingly clear and contemporary) writing of Sun Tzu, who so impressed Mao Tse-Tung. Much of Mao's strategic thought was inspired by Sun Tzu; and Vo Nguyen Giap, in turn, was a totally committed disciple of Mao. So similar are the writings of Mao and Giap that were their names removed from their works, a novice to the field would have difficulty differentiating their works or, in places, determining that they had different authors.

The Vietnamese Communists war was similar to the Chinese Communists anti-Fascist war against the Japanese (and to an extent against the Kuomintang). The theories and practices of united fronts, protracted war, political indoctrination of the army and the people, the advancement from guerrilla to mobile warfare came out of the Chinese experience. The Chinese war, like its successors in Vietnam, was a revolutionary war, in which political action was not only an element as important as military action but also a prerequisite to military victory.

In Sun Tzu's part of the world, immediately prior to the full-scale introduction of U.S. combat forces into South Vietnam in the spring of 1965, the government of the Republic of Vietnam was on its last legs. Although supplemented by cadres of specialists from the DRV, the indigenous Viet Cong main force units—battalions and regiments coalesced from scattered and smaller independent units—had defeated the South Vietnamese and had Saigon on the verge of collapse. That is why American combat troops were introduced into Vietnam at that time. It remains a subject of debate as to when the first People's Army of Vietnam (PAVN) troops appeared in the South; but by the end of 1965, there were only half a dozen PAVN regiments in the South, heavily outnumbered and outgunned by their American counterparts.

Nevertheless, by the time U.S. troops arrived in 1965, the Vietnamese Communists already controlled large sections of the south. The Communists, through their main forces, regional troops, and militia, had the South Vietnamese armed forces on the defensive, had disrupted the successors to strategic hamlet program, exercised political control (and contested control) over large areas, collected taxes, had eliminated thousands of members of South Vietnam's political and administrative apparatus throughout the country, had destroyed selected targets in the hearts of the major cities (including Saigon), and had closely tied their political and military strategies. These accomplishments were not the work of regular troops; by any measurement, this was *revolutionary warfare*.

Why could not the U.S. armed forces, especially the Army, understand this? It is something of a mystery, given the many Chinese and Vietnamese writings on the subject (not to mention the writings of Western experts). Although all kinds of specialists from the Chinese and Vietnamese Politburo and Central Military Committees to Sir Robert Thompson had described and analyzed revolutionary war in Vietnam, many U.S. Army officers focused on a single layer of this multilayered cake—the involvement of the regular (main force) units—and denounced counterinsurgency doctrine as irrelevant. They were gripped by the sight of Communist tanks bursting into the South Vietnamese presidential compound in April 1975, which seemed to prove their point that the real problem was enemy conventional warfare—a view not shared by the Communist victors.

James Clavell (author of *King Rat*, *Shogun*, *Tai-Pan*, and *Noble House*) has written that had Sun Tzu been read and understood by responsible political and military officials

Vietnam could not have happened as it happened; we would not have lost the war in Korea (we lost because we did not achieve victory); the Bay of Pigs could not have occurred; the hostage fiasco in Iran would not have come to pass; the British Empire would not have been dismembered; and, in all probability, World Wars I and II would have been avoided—certainly they would not have been waged as they were waged, and the millions of youths obliterated unnecessarily and stupidly by monsters calling themselves generals would have lived out their lives.[9]

Clavell has articulated what some military officers have long thought:

I would like to make *The Art of War* obligatory study for all our serving officers and men, as well as for all politicians and all people in government and all high schools and universities in the free world. If I were a commander in chief or president or prime minister I would go further: I would have written into law that all officers, *particularly all generals*, take a yearly oral and written examination on these thirteen chapters, the passing mark being 95 per cent—any general failing to achieve a pass to be automatically and summarily dismissed without appeal, and all other officers to have automatic demotion.[10]

Sun Tzu warned of the pitfalls incurred when a sovereign (or president) interferes with the conduct of military campaigns, and he cautioned commanders not to be pushed by the sovereign into bad strategies. He wrote that winning one's objective without having to fight was the acme of political-military skills; he saw no point in fighting (and wasting troops) for its own sake. Sun Tzu further warned against being drawn into a protracted war, noting among other things the enormous drain on the treasury imposed by military campaigns. (The United States is still suffering from the economic burdens of the long Vietnam War.)

Perhaps most important, Sun Tzu, more than two and one-half millennia ago, knew what too many senior American generals did not—namely, that commanding military forces is not the same as managing a political administration or a civilian business enterprise. Yet during the last three decades, our generals have become extraordinarily preoccupied with the concept of corporate management, and thousands of officers have received academic management degrees. Thus, General William Westmoreland was a graduate of the Harvard Business School, an institution obviously not attended by Vo Nguyen Giap or Van Tieng Dung (who, from their respective writings, gave no hint of ever receiving any management training at all). In the last analysis, the smaller and weaker fighters drove the bigger and more powerful managers from the mainland of Southeast Asia.

Sun Tzu also laid the groundwork for Tet and Khe Sanh. He acknowledged the supremacy of guile and secrecy: ''O divine art of subtely and secrecy! Through you we learn to be invisible, through you inaudible, and hence we can hold the enemy's fate in our hands.''[11] In the same vein, he stated: ''If we wish to fight, the enemy can be forced to an engagement even though he be sheltered behind high ramparts. . . . All we need to do is to attack some other place that he will be obliged to relieve.''[12] This was precisely what Giap and the Central Military Committee did in 1967–68. They attacked Khe Sanh, trapping a couple of U.S. Marine regiments although at huge costs to the Communists. President Johnson frantically ordered the Joint Chiefs of Staff to promise him that Khe Sanh would not fall (as had Dien Bien Phu) to the enemy. A large percentage of American ground and air power was diverted to support Khe Sanh (which we now know was not the object of destruction by the Communists), and much of the South was left open to increased PAVN and Viet Cong infiltration. These growing communist forces moved into position and attacked their enemy behind their "high ramparts" and in their "sheltered places," including the U.S. Embassy in Saigon. This stratagem of Sun Tzu brought them victory.

We could go on at some length in the same vein, but the point should be clear: this was Sun Tzu's kind of war, a war not known by Clausewitz. Apart from anything else, it was American cultural weaknesses that prevented the United States from devising sound strategies and tactics in the war.

THE KEY AXIOM: ATTACK THE ENEMY'S STRATEGY

For our purposes here, perhaps the key thought of Sun Tzu is this: "Thus, what is of supreme importance in war is to attack the enemy's strategy.''[13] The United States failed to do this in Vietnam, largely because of serious deficiencies in the knowledge and competence of senior American civilian and military officials. Even now, after such a calamity as befell the Americans in Indochina, the best that some can do is to point to the tactical battles won and ignore the larger lessons of Vietnam. Thus, in our military services today, practically nothing is heard of revolutionary war. The emphasis is on high technology and space—costly systems which, in financial terms, could slowly bring the United States to its knees.

In Vietnam, Americans ignored Sun Tzu and failed to attack the enemy's strategy. But the enemy heeded Sun Tzu: they attacked American strategy, building alliances that outflanked the administration in Washington and devising tactics to negate search-and-destroy military operations.

Repeatedly, the Communists have written of the the imperative of taking aim at the ''contradictions'' in the enemy ranks. And there were targets aplenty in both the Republic of Vietnam and the United States. Propagandizing and seeking to unite various dissident and protest groups in both the United States and South Vietnam was a primary task of the North Vietnamese. The apparent injustices and inequalities in American society—the splits between ethnic groups, the racism felt by some minorities, the unfairness of the draft, the problem of the diverging classes of rich and poor, the growing army of the homeless, and more— were grist for the mills of mass movements, civil disobedience, and protest. Police and security forces in selected parts of the United States were at times stretched to the breaking point, and a powerful incumbent President Johnson was broken and forced to retire from public life over the widespread unrest caused by the war. This societal dissonance was a portion of revolutionary warfare extended to the United States.

Summers in *On Strategy* perhaps also has underestimated the "friction" generated by the American news media, whose reporting—as differentiated from the war itself—was often less than ethically defensible. From Harrison Salisbury of the staff of *The New York Times* (who seemingly swallowed whole the propaganda fed to them by the Hanoi regime) to the scores of "stringers" in the more comfortable environs of Saigon, the American people received a great deal of subtle (and unsubtle) bias with the news. Professor P. J. Honey of London University's School of Oriental and African Studies has written in retrospect:

In my opinion, the American media lost the war through total incompetence and irresponsibility. We won in the Falklands, mainly by excluding the media until it was all over; and, if the United States had had any sense, it would have done the same thing in Vietnam.[14]

Given the level of intent and intelligence generally displayed by the Western news media, it is doubtful that even General Clausewitz himself could have succeeded in Vietnam.[15]

Colonel Summers devotes a considerable number of pages in his book to Clausewitz's concept of "centers of gravity." Clausewitz wrote that reducing the enemy's centers of gravity depends *foremost* on aiming at the enemy's political power. Success in this area is easiest to accomplish, wrote Clausewitz, when the enemy's distribution of "political power lies in the armed forces of a single government." It becomes increasingly difficult if powerful allies align themselves with the enemy, and they are "bound together by a common interest." The North Vietnamese were bound to powerful allies by common interests, all of which centered around the defeat and humiliation of the United States.

It has been often said that more conventional military measures would have defeated North Vietnam; that is, severe early bombing of the north, mining the harbors, and invasion of the Democratic Republic of Vietnam (DRV) would have crushed that government. The truth is that the North would have been militarily defeated, but any such victory would have been temporary at best. Assuming that its powerful socialist friends would not have intervened, North Vietnam probably could have been forced to agree to a cease-fire and at least a partial withdrawal of their regular forces from the south. Then what? The security of South Vietnam depended on the presence of American troops in greater than "advisory" numbers and on continuing American war supplies. How long could the Americans have stayed in strength? Two years? Ten years? Twenty years? The fact is that no large American garrison was possible without U.S. vital interests being directly involved; and once withdrawn, the South would have again been open to infiltration and invasion. And had a South Vietnamese leader done what would have been necessary to mobilize the state, the American press corps would have helped the DRV even more by their rush to expose his "brutal" and "corrupt" regime in Saigon. Clausewitz only goes so far.

WHAT IF THE UNITED STATES HAD INVADED NORTH VIETNAM?

Harry Summers, along with many others, makes much about the failure to attack North Vietnam with land forces. Here we might look back to Korea. Just as Clausewitz stated when talking about the attacker, when the U.S. forces drove to the Yalu in 1950, they became considerably weaker, their strength dissipated. Then the Chinese forces were able to defeat them and drive them back to the vicinity of the demarcation line, where the battle seesawed for the rest of the war. Therefore, as noted earlier, Korea was not an American victory, for one of the American objectives was the reunification of Korea under Syngman Rhee. By its defeat in the North, the United States was unable to accomplish this, so that only one of the American aims—the preservation of the South—was achieved.

Let us assume that the United States felt compelled to invade the Democratic Republic of Vietnam. What then? According to Clausewitz, the United States needed a big battle in order to destroy the Communist forces and gain victory. But would the Communists have offered Americans the big set-piece battle so arduously sought for decades by both the French and Americans? History suggests that the United States would have been disappointed and that the North Vietnamese would have retreated into the interior, or to China, where they would have had the advantage of secure base areas. It is not being facetious to say that unlike the Americans and most of their allied troops, Communist soldiers could walk long distances. Without vehicles, the U.S. Army comes to a halt.

And would the North Vietnamese people stand idly by as the aggressors pushed their way into their homeland? Would their Chinese allies stand by as an American army invaded a neighboring socialist state? The answers to these questions sobered even the most hawkish circles in Washington.

However, let us assume that the conditions specified by those Americans who saw an invasion of North Vietnam as necessary for victory were indeed present: Congress had declared war, the American people were indignant about North Vietnamese acts and fired up to fight for victory, the Clausewitzian frictions were lessened, and U.S. forces, applying their principles of war, went straight for the enemy's centers of gravity. Even disregarding U.S. commitments elsewhere, would there have been enough American troops available to carry out operations throughout Indochina? Assuming that no massive intervention of nearby Chinese Communist forces occurred, the People's Army of Vietnam was as large in numbers as any invading American force would have been (and probably larger), and the terrain of North Vietnam, outside the river deltas and lowlands, was made for defense and would have negated to some extent the American technological superiority. The borders with the People's Republic of

China (PRC) could not have been completely sealed, and U.S. forces would perhaps have claimed an empty capital.

Pursuit of the People's Army of Vietnam would have lengthened the U.S. lines of communications, and the American casualty rates would have skyrocketed. One look at the harsh ground found in much of Tonkin would have cooled the most ardent proponent of invading the North. With their ingrained philosophy of mobile warfare, combined with the kind of political control exercised by the Communists, plus the active sanctuary of China, the North Vietnamese would have shifted their old centers of gravity (as described by Clausewitz). Specifically and repeatedly the Chinese and Vietnamese Communists have rejected the positional warfare of Clausewitz.

Furthermore, let us suppose that the U.S. expeditionary forces would have cleared the Tonkin deltas of the PAVN, regional, and militia forces. What then? How large would the American occupation force have to be, and how long would it have to stay?

It seems likely that invading Tonkin in the 1960s would have been proportionately almost as costly in American casualties as projected casualties in invading Honshu in 1945. While an American victory may have been possible, in the long run the American invaders must eventually depart. The communists would have once again harnessed themselves to the irresistible twin engines of patriotism and independence and would have returned.

This scenario of an American invasion of North Vietnam is more than idle speculation. In 1954, the U.S. Army developed a concept plan by which the United States could intervene in support of the beleagured French Expeditionary Corps in Tonkin. This "Outline Plan for Conducting Military Operations in Indochina" (Tonkin) was commonly known as the Gavin Plan (named after Lieutenant General James Gavin).[16] Because the plan was published in 1954, only eleven years before U.S. combat troops intervened in strength in Annam and Cochin China, it would be useful to examine the strategy and assumptions contained in it.

The mission of U.S. ground forces invading Tonkin, as stated in the Gavin Plan, was to conduct military operations in Indochina in order to

* destroy organized enemy forces;

* establish conditions that would permit the Associated States to assume complete responsibility for their internal security;

* and establish conditions that would permit development of autonomous indigenous governments oriented to the West.

The naïveté, if not ignorance, revealed by the Pentagon in these mission objectives is startling. The deteriorating situation in Tonkin was caused as much by irregular warfare as by conventionally organized military units. These latter units—battalions, regiments, and divisions—had only been in existence for about four years and had been formed only after the smaller mobile units had created conditions favorable to the general Communist offensive. They could immediately be dismantled and converted back to smaller independent groups should the strategic position become unfavorable to the larger organized units.

Moreover, it was simply unrealistic to expect the Associated States to be able to compete fully—militarily or politically—with the Vietminh. Finally, the U.S. government itself—through a group of Office of Strategic Services (OSS) officers in Tonkin in 1944–45—aided in the ascendancy of the communists by openly siding with Ho Chi Minh's movement. All potential rivals to the communists were liquidated before and after the so-called August Revolution, not uncommonly with both the knowledge and the support of the OSS, so that eleven years later there was no possibility of establishing an "indigenous government oriented to the West."

Assumptions within the military plan were equally revealing. Two of the four assumptions stated that "Chinese Communist Forces will intervene overtly in Indochina" and that "atomic weapons will be used by friendly forces." Vietminh forces were estimated at nearly 300,000, of which 113,000 were regulars. There were 300,000 Chinese Communist troops in southern China, and their leading elements could reach the Red River delta seven days after their debarkation. Of the one-half million French Union Forces, only 94,500 were mobile combat forces; the rest were in static defense positions or were paramilitary personnel.

It would take five months to build up and concentrate U.S. forces, which would be built around seven and one-third infantry divisions, of which only one was judged combat-ready at the time. Total Army expeditionary strength would be 275,000. The plan assumed the mobilizing of a number of American National Guard and Reserve divisions and supporting units, while accepting the possibility that the Tonkin invasion might result in World War III or at least renewed Communist fighting on the recently quieted battlefield of Korea (or at Hong Kong). U.S. forces would first secure the Red River delta, then attack the Vietminh bases on the Chinese border. The plan acknowledged serious airlift and logistical problems.

A decade later, on the other side, the now stronger North Vietnamese recognized that an American invasion of the North, though unlikely, was not an impossibility. General Vo Nguyen Giap, then Defense Minister, stated in 1967 that the entire nation would be turned into an armed camp composed of three groups of forces: main force regular units, regional troops, and paramilitary local forces (grouped by functional area as local guerrillas, self-defense forces, combat village defense troops, and so on). Thus we see that the three main groups or classes of forces found in the South (main force units, Regional Forces, and Popular Forces) were mirrored in the North. The main difference lay in the tighter political control and indoctrination of the communist forces.

Giap stated that "the self-defense militia is a strategic force in our people's armed revolutionary struggles."[17] He regarded these groups as "an invincible force, the iron wall of the fatherland."[18] Giap noted that during the anti-French war the Vietminh self-defense militia and guerrilla forces were "the largest armed forces." He never separated the three main classes of troops.

1979: WHAT THE CHINESE LEARNED (AGAIN)

Again, we can do more than speculate on how the North Vietnamese might have reacted to an American invasion of Tonkin, because in February 1979, Tonkin *was invaded* by the Chinese People's Liberation Army. The Chinese, in their words, hoped to "teach the Vietnamese a lesson" and punish Vietnam for invading Kampuchea. When the fighting was over, there was some confusion as to who was the real recipient of the lesson. Although news reporting was sparse, there were indications that the Chinese had a more difficult time than expected. The fighting revealed a rustiness in Chinese fighting techniques, reflecting the relatively long period between China's last major test (Korea) and the 1979 battle. The Vietnamese, who had been fighting continuously during the same period, provided to be formidable foes. Furthermore, the shock waves of Chinese regulars apparently were met not by Vietnamese regular main force divisions but by reinforced regional and local self-defense troops. The Vietnamese elite main force divisions were deployed around Hanoi and the delta regions, ready to hit the Chinese forces if and when they fought through the regional forces. The Chinese withdrew before engaging the bulk of the Vietnamese main forces.

From this Chinese experience, we may develop a likely scenario for the Vietnamese Communist response to an American invasion of Tonkin. Massed guns and missiles would have challenged the preceding air attacks, while troop landings would have been met by reinforced regional and local forces, who would be defending their own land and villages. As the fighting heated up and the American lines of communication were lengthened, the People's Army of Vietnam would have struck to cut selected vulnerable American lines of communication in order to encircle and attack targeted U.S. troop concentrations. The Communist objective would have been to kill large numbers of American troops. All of these developments would have been bad enough, but the likelihood would remain that the Chinese Army would swarm down from the North to catch surviving Americans between the Vietnamese, the Chinese, the mountains, and the sea.

Finally, what about unleashing the full fury of American air power against the North while simultaneously mining the major ports and cutting the Ho Chi Minh road system with troops? The North's ability to continue to fight would have been severely impaired, and the country could have been brought to the breaking point. But the borders with China could never be sealed, and the Vietnamese have done tremendous logistical feats by mobilizing masses of people and pointing them in the right direction. Moreover, unremitting, indiscriminate American air attacks would have taken their place beside Guernica and Rotterdam, as My Lai has joined Lidice and other scenes of atrocities. Would the ends have justified the terrible costs involved?

Let us assume further that all of the above tactics worked and that the Vietnamese Communists—very stubborn people—threw in the towel. How long would it have been before they would have picked it up again? How long could the Americans have remained to enforce their victory?

Had Clausewitz been alive in our time and serving as an American general during the Vietnam years, he too probably would have lost this war. His theory demands a target, an enemy army to destroy, and the Communists would not have offered him such a target. His principles of war would have meant little. Even if American forces had invaded North Vietnam, the Communists would have offered U.S. forces no tempting centers of gravity at which to strike. The government and the army would have retreated to their original revolutionary base areas, and then to China if necessary, leaving the masses to wage a relentless people's war against the invading troops—in the manner of the Spaniards against Napoleon's invading army.

In the end, the United States needed new theories and new strategies to wage the war it found in Indochina. Recent history suggests that the United States has yet to master, or perhaps even understand, irregular warfare.

NOTES

1. The comparisons between the limited wars fought in Korea and Indochina may not be valid; the dissimilarities outweigh the similarities. We may also disagree with the assertion that Korea was an American victory; presumably this argument rests on the fact that the Republic of Korea was preserved. But this was only part of the American objective, for after Inchon, U.S. (and UN) policy added the goal of reunifying Korea as an anticommunist state; this aim was defeated by Communist China.

2. As cited in Bernard Fall, *Street Without Joy: Indochina at War, 1946–54* (Harrisburg, Pa.: Stackpole, 1964), p. 34.

3. For an account of the final campaign of the war between North and South Vietnam, see Senior General Van Tien Dung, *Our Great Spring Victory: An Account of the Liberation of South Vietnam*, translated by John Spragens Jr. (New York: Monthly Review Press, 1977).

4. As cited in Harry G. Summers, Jr. *On Strategy: The Vietnam War in Context* (New York: Dell, 1984), p. 122.

5. For Mao's discussion of revolutionary war strategy and philosophy, see, for example, *Selected Military Writings of Mao Tse-tung* (Peking: Foreign Language Press, 1967), and *On Revolution and War*, edited by M. Rejai (Garden City, N.Y.: Doubleday, 1969).

6. B. H. Liddell Hart in Sun Tzu's *The Art of War*, translated by Samuel Griffith (New York: Oxford University Press, 1977), pp. v-vii.

7. For a concise discussion of the U.S. military effort in Vietnam, see Peter Dunn, "The American Army: The Vietnam War, 1965–1973," in *Armed Forces and Modern Counterinsurgency*, edited by Ian Beckett and John Pimlott (London: Croom, Helm, 1985).

8. Karl von Clausewitz, *On War*, edited and translated by Michael Howard and Peter Paret (Princeton, N.J.: Princeton University Press, 1976), p. 220.

9. Sun Tzu, *The Art of War*, edited by James Clavell (reprint; New York: Delacorte Press, 1983), p. 2.

10. Ibid., p. 7.

11. Ibid., p. 26.

12. Ibid.

13. Sun Tzu, *Art of War*, Griffith translation, p. 77.

14. P. J. Honey, letter to author, 28 May 1985. Honey states:

Not one single American correspondent spoke, read, or understood any Vietnamese at all. Tran Bach Dang, Central Committee member of the Communist Party who was in charge of "Dan Van" (civil affairs) and "Tri-Thuc Van" (intellectual affairs) for Saigon/Cholon, latched on to that fact very early on and moved heaven and earth to secure English-speaking Communist agents to act as guide-interpreters to the U.S. press. These people influenced correspondents, misrepresented and fabricated "news" to an unbelievable extent and virtually dictated what the U.S. people should read and see about the war. One of the agents, Pham Xuan An, who first worked with Reuters, later transferred to *Time* and was eventually promoted to full *Time* correspondent. At the same time, he was living with an American female correspondent in Saigon. He is now a very senior official in Vietnam, and I learn that he was fairly recently being considered for the post of ambassador to the United Nations. He was finally passed over because it was thought that, when he was recognized by all his former American friends, the truth of his earlier role might leak out, and that would be counterproductive.

15. Appearing on the ABC television program "45/85" in September 1985, Arkady Shevchenko—a high ranking Soviet political defector—said that while in Moscow he had been present at a Politburo meeting in which Yuri Andropov stated that the war would be won by the Communists: the demonstrations resulting from the stirring up of the American public would ensure an American defeat.

16. "Outline Plan for Conducting Military Operations in Indochina" (1954), in U.S. National Archives, Record Group 319, Records of the Army Staff.

17. "General Vo Nguyen Giap on the Strategic Role of the Self-Defense Militia," in *Visions of Victory: Selected Vietnamese Communist Military Writings, 1964–1968*, edited by Patrick J. McGarvey (Stanford, California: Hoover Institution Press, 1969), p. 169.

18. Ibid., p. 170.

8

Noel C. Eggleston

On Lessons: A Critique of the Summers Thesis

> The lessons of history are never simple. Whoever thinks he sees one should probably keep on with his reading.
> —John K. Fairbank

Postwar analysis of a conflict like Vietnam is welcome and, in any case, inevitable. History that is speculative, or what may also be termed counterfactual, is interesting but perhaps a more questionable exercise. While it does not always "drive historians wild," as Colonel Harry Summers states, it should concern us especially when it is presented as an objective proposition free of the prejudices of past studies.[1] It is safe in the sense that the author, though he can be attacked, cannot be proven "wrong"; no one can know what might have happened if leaders had formulated policy or strategy in a different manner. Yet it can lead toward a refusal to accept negative results and a failure to recognize lessons that might have been learned.

We seem to have reached a period in America today in which society has been able to leave behind some of the bitterness and antagonism of the past as people have come to grips with the Vietnam War. On the whole this healing process is undoubtedly healthy for America—we can witness a near full emergence from the closet of the Vietnam veteran and a willingness even to honor those who fought in an unpopular war; the beginnings of a commitment to deal with the problems that remain for the veteran; an interest in exploring the Vietnam War through academic courses; and a foreign policy less characterized by knee-jerk reactions to the past war but still possessing a caution born of careful consideration concerning the mistakes made.

Yet the new spirit also carries worrisome overtones. The young generation of camouflage-clad students nurtured on the likes of Rambo and Chuck Norris know little of the real Vietnam War. They are joined by others from the Vietnam era who want to—perhaps need to—believe that the war was an aberration and that America was and is still number one (whatever that phrase means). This search for redemption magnifies every American action in the world. In this victory-starved atmosphere the simple forcing down of a terrorist-bearing Egyptian airplane takes on the air of a significant diplomatic and military victory for America; a bombing raid on Libya assumes the dimensions of a wartime success. For these groups, stab-in-the-back theories, in which the true villains are spineless politicians and left-leaning journalists, offer convenient explanations for America's ultimate troubles in Vietnam and leave hope that Vietnam was in the end a winnable war—its leaders at the time simply were not winners.

Some of the new "revisionist" writing on Vietnam, which argues on behalf of the morality and winnability of the war, feeds, I fear, these feelings. I do not wish to simplify Colonel Harry Summers's sophisticated work and would certainly not place him in the stab-in-the-back school. Indeed, he levies most of the blame he finds on the military itself and warns against the dangers of blaming the media and overemphasizing the problems of political interference. Yet I would suggest that one basis for the apparent large popularity of his book is a basic implication that it carries—that the United States could have won in Vietnam if we had just done things differently. It is a message that many have been waiting to hear for over ten years, and I can personally see it's warm reception by my students in the classroom. It gives me some reason for concern.

Colonel Summers's discussion of America's political and strategic conduct in Vietnam has drawn much criticism from those with military and political expertise on the war, and before I add my share to it, I would like to applaud those areas where I feel he has made a significant contribution. Summers's ideas on Vietnam have become familiar to students of the war.[2] Briefly, Summers compares the decision making and conduct of the Vietnam War with the theoretical principles set forth by military theorist Karl von Clausewitz in his classic study *On War*. In a review of "The Environment," Summers examines the "National Will" as expressed through the people and Congress, and the concept of "Friction" between the Army and the people, within the bureaucracy, over the alleged dangers of China and nuclear war, and over doctrine, especially counterinsurgency. He also studies "The Engagement" through Clausewitz's framework of tactics and strategy; the objective; the offensive; mass, economy of force, and maneuver; unity of command; security and surprise; simplicity; and coalition warfare. Summers finds America's performance wanting in almost every category.

I have found some of Summers's well-written, well-organized, and well-argued points quite persuasive. His general assessment on the necessity of committing the American people to war—something he argues was not done in the Vietnam conflict—seems to me on target (though I will question the specific means to this end in the 1964–65 context shortly.) According to Summers, by sanitizing the conflict, by trying to fight it "in cold blood" with no declaration of war, no mobilization, no tax increase, and the use of student deferments,

President Lyndon Johnson sacrificed long-range success for short-term consensus. Feeling uncommitted to the military effort, a divided public often turned on the military rather than on policymakers when the war went downhill. With no clear sense of purpose and no consciously given ties to the war, American citizens were also unwilling to support a seemingly indefinite conflict with uncertain goals. It seems to me wiser to abide by the general principle voiced in *On Strategy* that "without the commitment of the American people the commitment of the Army to prolonged combat was"—and I assume Summers would say is—"impossible." Moreover, this method of approaching war requires that American leaders make the price of involvement clear.[3] For Summers this can be done in limited way for a limited war; mobilization of public opinion does not have to be geared toward a total war concept. I might add one caveat here—the war best be limited also in terms of time and setbacks, for patience does not seem to be the American public's strongest virtue when it sees few results despite extensive efforts expended.

His stress on the importance of creating concise, understandable objectives and a clear definition of victory is another point worthy of consideration though I find some imbalance here in his judgment of North Vietnamese success and American failure. According to Summers, "American political objectives were never clear during the entire course of the war."[4] It does seem evident that so many rationales were offered over the years that specific goals might have been lost for the public in the confusion and that consequently the American people might not have had a clear perception of exactly why we were in Vietnam. Yet John Gates's critique on this point is of interest. He argues that American goals were in fact clearer than Summers claims; the problem as Gates sees it was more in the realm of how to achieve those goals.[5] Summers does appear willing to accept as North Vietnam's goal its rather broad plan to conquer and communize South Vietnam. One could make a strong case that the similarly broad American goal of an independent, noncommunist South Vietnam, friendly to the United States and reasonably democratic, remained a consistent element of policy from 1954 to 1973. I fail to see a difference of astuteness at this level.

In a broad sense, Summers's detailed analysis of strategy versus tactics and America's confusion of the two is also for me a worthy aspect of his work. According to Summers, while North Vietnam carried out a strategic offensive and varied between tactical offensive and tactical defensive maneuvers as the situation warranted, the United States confused its strategy with tactics. Specifically, military leaders misread the tactical offensive for a strategic offensive and instead ended up pursuing a defensive strategy with a "negative" aim of wearing down the enemy. The failure of the military to understand this problem, a result of generally muddled thinking, neglect of military strategy since World War II, and a fascination with counterinsurgency left them unable to warn civilian leaders of the inevitable problems that would result.

As an alternative Summers argues that using our defense of Korea as a model—a point stressed repeatedly in his work (and I have geographical, historical, and interpretive problems with a direct comparison of Korea and Vietnam)—we could and should have recognized that the strategic defensive combined with a tactical offensive was the best method of containing the expansion of North Vietnam, for him the real enemy. For Summers this policy could have preserved the status quo, prevented the enemy from reaching its goal, and provided the basis for negotiation. While I have serious reservations concerning his specific alternatives, it does seem to me Summers has performed a service in placing part of the debate on this broad theoretical ground of analysis.

While a number of other valuable points appear in his analysis of the more specific categories of mass, economy of force, maneuver, simplicity, and unity of command, I would like to focus on one further broad argument effectively voiced by Summers. In my study of the war I have come to feel as Colonel Summers does that the military was asked to take on responsibilities in the areas of counterinsurgency and nation-building that were and are best left to the peoples intimately involved in the struggle. As General Fred C. Weyand argued in 1976: "the military [was] being called upon to perform political, economic, and social tasks beyond its capability."[6] If the hosts are capable of creating a viable nation and combating insurgents, then the United States may be able to add vital assistance to their efforts; if they cannot, then the United States simply cannot do it for them. "Ludicrous" and "self-defeating" are two of the words Summers uses to describe American attempts to win the "hearts and minds" of the Vietnamese people. They are harsh words, but as he points out in an article in *The New Republic*, in a sense the more success the United States might have had in this area, the greater potential there would have been for creating more alienation between the Vietnamese people and their government in the long run.[7] A certain arrogance characteristic of the early and mid–1960s, perhaps most ably described by David Halberstam in *The Best and the Brightest*, convinced us we could do all things in Vietnam including establish a nation.[8] Our actual experience there demonstrated, however, that while American forces could help destroy an enemy, they could not create loyalty, confidence, or a mandate of heaven for a government. As I will mention shortly, I am not convinced the South Vietnamese leaders of that time could have either, but it seems to me that whatever final results occur must be the product of internal forces. This point gives me pause when I see critics of the war argue that a massive American-directed counterinsurgency or pacification program would have been the answer to U.S. problems in Vietnam. This seems to me a trap comparative to that into which supporters of a strict military solution fall; that is, that the war required an American-dominated response. While much of Summers's general analysis of America's role in Vietnam has stirred thinking and generated debate, his suggestion of an alternative strategy for victory has created quite a storm. And it is here I would like to turn; it is here also that I find my support for his ideas considerably lessened.

Summers's thesis springs from parts of his analysis already mentioned. As he views it, Vietnam was not the scene of a revolutionary civil war. Though he describes the First Indochina War as a revolutionary conflict, the second war was in its essence a conventional war planned, directed, and largely executed by North Vietnam with only a ''smoke screen facade'' of guerrilla war carried out by its deceived ally, the Viet Cong. Summers argues that American military and political leaders did not recognize this and consequently went chasing after Viet Cong shadows with a debilitating policy of counterinsurgency. In the process we so Americanized the war that the South Vietnamese were left with little role to play. With apologies to General Omar Bradley, we fought in Summers's view the wrong type of war (counterinsurgency), in the wrong places (all over South Vietnam), at perhaps the right, or at least necessary, time, but with the wrong enemy (the Viet Cong.)

Based on these assumptions, Summers suggests that the correct strategy would have been to place American troops along the Demilitarized Zone and across Laos. Rallying the American people through mobilization and a declaration of war to support the military effort, this force would have been used as a shield to prevent North Vietnamese infiltration and to contain communism. Behind this shield South Vietnam would have been charged with the tasks of destroying the Viet Cong insurgency (with some early American help), as well as of pacification, and of building a viable nation.

In Summers's scenario the American public would have accepted this limited peacekeeping role especially since the costs in terms of men and money would have been relatively low. It would have avoided some of the more troublesome issues of the war such as the search-and-destroy tactics and the bombing of populated areas. It would have forced North Vietnam to become the aggressor, and should an attack have taken place, the battles would have played to America's strength of massive firepower. With the North Vietnamese contained, South Vietnam would have been able to handle the Viet Cong who would have been left in General Bruce Palmer's words—from whom Summers borrows and/or shares much—''to wither on the vine.''[9]

It is a provocative thesis, but there are many areas open to serious question. I will limit myself to three broad areas of objection. First, I have problems with Colonel Summers's perception of the type of war being fought and his non-recognition of the historical context of 1964–1965. Writers including Russell Weigley, John Gates, Guenter Lewy, Paul Kattenberg, Hung Nguyen, and Timothy Lomperis have recently stressed that while there was a conventional military side to the war, as witnessed in the 1972 and 1975 offensives, it *was* a revolutionary war with a major guerilla element that cannot be overlooked.[10] I agree with John Gates when he argues that ''any analysis that denies the important revolutionary dimensions of the Vietnam conflict is misleading.''[11] Though Summers implies that he sees a mixed bag of war types from 1965 to 1968, he essentially views the Viet Cong as an auxilliary force without apparent revolutionary goals. He accepts a narrow definition of a ''classic revolutionary war'' and allows no role for the Vietnamese ability to blend models.[12] To support his theory, he ends up concentrating heavily on the 1972 and 1975 offensives. As he states in *On Strategy*: "In retrospect, our entire approach to the war would have been different if at the beginning we could have foreseen the North Vietnamese tanks rumbling through the streets of Saigon on 1 May 1975."[13] A core question is this: Does this reading of history backwards hold up? Because the war ended on a conventional note, does that mean it was like that from the start and was devoid of revolutionary aspects? I would argue that Colonel Summers has misread the *types* of war that occurred and underestimated the second "center of gravity" that was present, the Viet Cong. While Summers argues that proof of the conventional nature of the war is the fact that after the Viet Cong was decimated in the Tet Offensive the war continued as before only without the guerrilla smoke screen, I would contend that even if North Vietnam had not begun troop infiltration in 1964, the Viet Cong would have been a viable military and political force in itself, albeit on a smaller scale.

To dismiss the Viet Cong—both the military force and the political program it represented—as a minor adjunct to the "real" threat from the north is to perpetuate in another fashion the underestimation of enemy forces so common by American leaders in the 1960s. It also undervalues the revolutionary philosophy offered by Ho, Giap, and other leaders of the revolution since the 1930s. As both John Gates and Russell Weigley argue, Vietnamese writings on the conduct of the war never claimed that the Viet Cong would win on its own.[14] But the final victory would bring the fall of the South Vietnamese regime and its replacement by a new revolutionary government. Cooperation of these forces, even gradual dominance by the North Vietnamese Army, did not automatically end the revolutionary political side of the war.

Summers might have made a stronger case had he stressed the changing nature of the war after 1968. Timothy Lomperis makes a telling point on this issue. In his book *The War Everyone Lost—and Won* he describes a People's War conducted from 1965–1968 that ultimately failed in the Tet Offensive of 1968. Like Summers, he sees a change toward conventional war, but one which came only *after* the decimation of the Viet Cong.[15] Even then the revolutionary goals continued.

A similar retort to the "wither-on-the-vine" school is offered by Lawrence Grinter. In a 1975 article entitled "How They Lost: Doctrines, Strategies and Outcomes of the Vietnam War," Grinter carefully analyzed six competing political-military strategies employed by various parties during the war. In criticizing what he calls America's predominant doctrine/strategy in Vietnam, the "Stability Operations plus Economic Development Approach," he includes an important point relative to this issue of war and revolution. It was a "fundamental error," he said, "to assume that the ultimate source of South Vietnam's problems lay not in the South but in the North." He adds: "By concentrating massive resources and effort against infiltration from the North rather than focusing on the political and administrative decay in the South [they] . . . missed the actual processes and dynamics by which the revolution endured".[16] So, I would suggest, does Harry Summers.

else's country forever.''[33] Would the public have been prepared for an indefinite stay of American troops? If the troops were removed, or a token force left, would the public have supported their return to South Vietnam? Would South Vietnam have been able to handle a renewal of North Vietnam's effort, which would have had an opportunity to increase its already formidable forces? And would the adaptable North Vietnamese leaders have remained blocked by the U.S. shield in the first place, or instead countered the Summers's strategy in ways other than a direct attack? Their record certainly demonstrates a calculated flexibility; Summers seems to assume a static response by the North Vietnamese that may well not be warranted. In a contest of national wills, I do not see America as having the edge in perserverance in Vietnam.

In response to one group of writers in his broad review of ''schools'' on the Vietnam War, George Herring notes: ''The conclusion that Vietnam was not susceptible to our will is not an easy one to accept.''[34] Neither was the final result of the Chinese Civil War. Yet even General Bruce Palmer has concluded:

Can a great power and a democracy wage war successfully against a small power and a totalitarian state, especially if that great power has a national conscience and is influenced and inhibited by ''world opinion''? Putting it in a different way, can a great power fight a limited war against a small power which is waging total war, especially if that country is being supported by large outside powers? Was it really practicable for the United States to fight a limited war against North Vietnam, whose war-making capabilities, other than manpower, were provided almost entirely by the Soviet Union and China? It seems to me that the answer lies closer to ''no'' than ''yes.''[35]

Perhaps an analysis of the Vietnam war should reinforce the fact that some events simply remain beyond the control of the United States. Not that this country should abandon friends or even refuse to make an effort when success looks unlikely—but to approach problems with a realistic view of what we can and cannot accomplish seems a reasonable goal for the future. On balance, Colonel Harry Summers has moved us in this direction with his analysis of America's role in Vietnam. He has forced us to reevaluate our perceptions of the war, to reconsider our evidence, and to reexamine the role that the Vietnam War should play in our future strategic thinking. If, as I feel, he has detoured from that positive path with his alternative scenario for victory, he has still given us much to contemplate and debate, and in the end our future policies should be better for it.

NOTES

1. Harry G. Summers, tr., ''Palmer, Karnow, and Herrington: A Review of Recent Vietnam War Historians,'' *Parameters* 15 (Spring 1985): 82; Summers, ''A Strategic Perspective of the Vietnam War,'' *Parameters* 13 (June 1983), p. 45.

2. Information on Summers's views is taken from the following sources: Harry G. Summers, Jr., *On Strategy* (Novato, Cal.: Presidio Press, 1982); Summers, ''Vietnam

Reconsidered," *The New Republic* 187 (July 12, 1982), pp. 25–31; Summers, "A Strategic Perspective of the Vietnam War," *Parameters* 13 (June 1983), pp. 41–46; Summers, "Palmer, Karnow, and Herrington," *Parameters* 15 (Spring 1985), pp. 77–83.

3. Summers, *On Strategy*, p. 13. On this point of "National Will," see Chapters 1 and 2. Norman Graebner lends his support to this idea of commitment. See Norman A. Graebner, "American Foreign Policy After Vietnam," *Parameters* 15 (Autumn 1985), p. 46.

4. Summers, *On Strategy*, p. 98.

5. John M. Gates, "Vietnam: The Debate Goes On," *Parameters* 14 (Spring 1984), pp. 15, 19–20.

6. Summers, *On Strategy*, p. 79.

7. Summers, "Vietnam Reconsidered," p. 27.

8. David Halberstam, *The Best and the Brightest* (New York: Random House, 1972).

9. See General Bruce Palmer, Jr., *The 25, Year War* (Lexington: University Press of Kentucky, 1984), pp. 182–186.

10. Russell Weigley, "Reflecting on 'Lessons' From Vietnam," in Peter Braestrup, ed., *Vietnam as History* (Washington, D.C.: University Press of America, 1984), pp. 115–124; Gates, "The Debate Goes On," pp. 15–25; Guenter Lewy, "Some Political-Military Lessons of the Vietnam War," *Parameters* 14 (Spring 1984), pp. 2–14 and Lewy, *America in Vietnam* (New York: Oxford University Press, 1978); Paul M. Kattenberg, "Reflections on Vietnam: Of Revisionism and Lessons Yet to be Learned," *Parameters* 14 (Autumn 1984), pp. 42–50; Hung P. Nguyen, "Communist Offensive Strategy and the Defense of South Vietnam," *Parameters* 14 (Winter 1984), pp. 3–19; Timothy Lomperis, *The War Everyone Lost—and Won* (Baton Rouge: Louisiana State University Press, 1984).

11. Gates, "The Debate Goes On," p. 23.

12. Summers, "Palmer, Karnow, and Herrington," p. 79; Summers, *On Strategy*, p. 76.

13. Summers, *On Strategy*, p. 85.

14. Gates, "The Debate Goes On," pp. 16–18; Weigley, " 'Lessons' from Vietnam," p. 120.

15. Lomperis, *The War Everyone Lost—And Won*, pp. 133–137, 147–151.

16. Lawrence E. Grinter, "How They Lost: Doctrines, Strategies and Outcomes of the Vietnam War," *Asian Survey* 15:12 (December 1975), 1129.

17. Douglas Pike, *PAVN: People's Army of Vietnam* (Novato, Cal.: Presidio Press, 1986), p. 251. On this point, also see pages 213–253.

18. Summers, *On Strategy*, pp. 23, 26.

19. Gary Hess, review essay on "The Military Perspective on Strategy in Vietnam: Harry G. Summers's *On Strategy* and Bruce Palmer's "The 25-Year War," *Diplomatic History* vol. 10, no. 1, (Winter 1986), p. 99.

20. John D. Stuckey and Joseph H. Pistorius, "Mobilization for the Vietnam War: A Political and Military Catastrophe," *Parameters* 15 (Spring 1985), pp. 36–37.

21. Larry Berman, *Planning a Tragedy* (New York: W. W. Norton & Company, 1982), p. 72.

22. Quoted in Lewy, *America in Vietnam*, p. 393.

23. On this issue, see Daniel S. Papp, *Vietnam: The View From Moscow, Peking, Washington* (Jefferson, N.C.: McFarland & Company, 1981), pp. 37–38, 40, 74–75; Herbert Y. Schandler, *Lyndon Johnson and Vietnam* (Princeton, N.J.: Princeton Uni-

versity Press, 1977), p. 34; Berman, *Planning a Tragedy*, pp. 71–72; Lyndon Johnson, *The Vantage Point* (New York: Holt, Rinehart and Winston, 1971), pp. 119, 131; George C. Herring, *America's Longest War*, revised edition, (New York: Alfred A. Knopf, 1986), pp. 125, 128, 132, 139, 145.

24. Berman, *Planning a Tragedy*, p. 149.

25. Summers, *On Strategy*, p. 86.

26. Ronald Spector, *Advice and Support: The Early Years, 1941–1960* (Washington, D.C.: Center of Military History, 1983). Other recent works which comment on ARVN are Palmer's, "The 25-Year War," pp. 57, 94, 101, 104; and Shelby L. Stanton, *The Rise and Fall of an American Army* (Novato, Cal.: Presidio Press, 1985), pp. 82–83.

27. On this general point, see Lomperis, *Lost—And Won*, p. 160; and George C. Herring, "American Strategy in Vietnam: The Postwar Debate," *Military Affairs* 46 (April 1982), pp. 57–63.

28. See, for example, Truong Nhu Tang, *A Viet Cong Memoir* (San Diego, Cal.: Harcourt, Brace, and Jovanovich, 1985).

29. Grinter, "How They Lost," pp. 1114–1132.

30. Summers, *On Strategy*, p. 18.

31. Charles M. Andrews, "The American Revolution: An Interpretation," *American Historical Review* vol. XXXI, No. 2 (January 1926), p. 232.

32. David Fromkin and James Chace, "What *Are* the Lessons of Vietnam?" *Foreign Affairs* 63 (Spring 1985), p. 734.

33. Weigley, " 'Lessons' from Vietnam," p. 123.

34. Herring, "American Strategy," p. 61.

35. Palmer, "The 25-Year War," p. 208.

V

THE WAR'S LEGACY FOR FUTURE U.S. CONFLICT PERFORMANCE

Revolutionary wars and insurrections, both Communist dominated and nationalist, broke out with such frequency in the 1970s and 1980s that it left United States defense planners little time to assess the reasons for our failure in Vietnam even if they had wanted to. Indeed, as Hanoi's Soviet-built tanks were knocking down Saigon's presidential office gates, much of the Third World was coming under revolutionary seige. As Indochina was collapsing, a major Soviet-Cuban airlift and sealift occurred, carrying 20,000 Cubans across the South Atlantic to combat in Angola 6,000 miles away. Angola was followed by Marxist takeovers in Mozambique, Guinea, Ethiopia, Afghanistan, and South Yemen; attempted coups in Sudan and Somalia; a probable Soviet-influenced assassination in North Yemen; increased Soviet military assistance and ties to Libya, Syria, Vietnam, Laos, and Cambodia; and, as Nicaragua collapsed, the emergence of a Soviet-Cuban beachhead on the mainland of Central America.

While all this was happening, the U.S. army published its long awaited, and revised, post-Vietnam War doctrine manual. Titled "Operations" and dated July 1976, Army Field Manual 100–5 concentrated exclusively on how to repel a Soviet/Warsaw Pact invasion of West Europe. The manual did not mention either the Vietnam War or the Army's 20-year experience in Indochina. The Air Force and the Navy also declared themselves ready to concentrate on strategic deterrence and high-technology conventional warfare.

Within the defense and foreign affairs community, however, a small group of determined officers and analysts refused to join the head-in-the-sand school of Vietnam "dropouts"; instead, they sought to probe the Vietnam experience thoroughly. Colonel Harry Summers is one of those iconoclasts. Another is Colonel John Waghelstein, a decorated Vietnam veteran and a soldier-scholar who commanded the U.S. military assistance team in El Salvador prior to taking command of the Army's 7th Special Forces Group. In his essay, "Countersurgency Doctrine and Low-Intensity Conflict in the Post-Vietnam Era," that follows, Colonel Waghelstein explores the Army's problems in coming to terms with the new era of low-intensity conflict and the broader resistance in the armed services in preparing for these kinds of wars, both intellectually and operationally. Categorizing low-intensity conflict as, in reality, revolutionary and counterrevolutionary warfare, Colonel Waghelstein states: ''It is *total war* at the grassroots level—one that uses *all* of the weapons of total war, including political, economic and psychological warfare with the military aspect being a distant fourth in many cases.'' His essay concludes with recommendations to make the U.S. armed services doctrine, organization, and education more relevant to this new era of conflict.

The book concludes with a final essay by Colonel Peter Dunn and Dr. Lawrence Grinter. Analyzing the findings and recommendations of the book's authors, the editors examine the intellectual, strategy, and organizational difficulties that the United States brought to its conduct of the Vietnam War and how the authors' recommendations might have corrected these problems. The editors then step back from the American war in Vietnam and forecast the kinds of problems and constraints that are likely to hamper U.S. performance in the next round of low-intensity conflicts it will be (or already has been) drawn into. The editors find their observations correlate fairly closely to the problems identified by the military reform movement in the United States. The post-Vietnam U.S. armed services show a military establishment fixated with high-technology and conventional war, career systems that deny promotions to low-intensity conflict specialists, the triumph of management over strategy (and the substitution of tactics for what little strategy thinking is done), the rise of huge military support and technocratic bureaucracies, and the continuing tendency to recast the nature of wars to fit preferred U.S. doctrine and strategy.

9

John D. Waghelstein

Counterinsurgency Doctrine and Low-Intensity Conflict in the Post-Vietnam Era

In the post-Vietnam era, counterinsurgency has virtually become a non-subject in the U.S. military educational system. The term *counterinsurgency* has been replaced by the less controversial *low-intensity conflict* (LIC). A recently proposed definition of low-intensity conflict for the revised Army field manual on that subject reads:

. . . the limited use of power for political purposes by nations or organizations . . . to coerce control or defend a population, to control or defend a territory or establish or defend rights. It includes military operations by or against irregular forces, peacekeeping operations, terrorism, counter-terrorism, rescue operations and military assistance under conditions of armed conflict. This form of conflict does not include protracted engagements of opposing regular forces.

The problem with this definition is that low-intensity conflict is a description of the level of violence from a military viewpoint. This kind of conflict is more accurately described as revolutionary and counterrevolutionary warfare. It is *total war* at the grass-roots level—one that uses *all* of the weapons of total war, including political, economic and psychological warfare with the military aspect being a distant fourth in many cases. The subordination of the military in counterinsurgency has always created problems for the U.S. military establishment. This kind of conflict is fundamentally different from the American way of war.

Low-intensity conflict and counterinsurgency involve two distinct uses of the U.S. military. The first, as demonstrated in the Grenada operation, is the surgical application of force—a role for which U.S. units are trained and equipped. The second use involves assisting an ally in politico-military operations to combat armed insurgents, a role for which the U.S. military is unprepared. The state of preparedness for this second role is at its lowest point in 20 years.

Low-intensity conflict instruction at the U.S. Army command and General

Staff College (USACGSC), Fort Leavenworth, Kansas, includes an analysis of insurgency—the causes, the catalysts and the role of the sponsor in generating insurgency as well as ways the United States can best *assist* besieged friendly governments in countering insurgencies. Developmental or consolidative campaigns aimed at the root causes of insurgency are studied as well as methods of mobilizing human and material resources and ways of neutralizing the armed guerrilla threat. In short, the doctrine stresses a balanced approach of development, mobilization, and neutralization.

Additionally, there is a careful analysis of various types of insurgencies and the social groups and political forces existing in each. Case studies are used (for example, Venezuela, 1959–63) as well as the macro approach. The situation-specific aspects of each insurgency are stressed to preclude another "cookie cutter" disaster—for example, trying to apply a Malayan strategic hamlet solution to Vietnam. What little doctrine there is is sound and provides some useful tools to those officers who may be called upon to operate in a counterinsurgency environment.

The real problem is not the doctrine but the amount of emphasis that the services place on the subject. For example, by 1977, a paltry 40 hours of the one-year-course core curriculum at the USACGSC were devoted to the study of low-intensity conflict. Two years later, the low-intensity conflict course had been reduced to 8 hours. In the branch school, the subject was discontinued altogether. The U.S. Army still does not regard guerrilla warfare, insurgency and counterinsurgency as being unique and is unwilling to devote substantial resources to preparing for our most likely form of involvement.

A recent study by Captain Andrew F. Krepenevitch of the Department of Social Sciences, U.S. Military Academy, West Point, New York, details the Army's failure in the early 1960s to make any serious attempt at developing counterinsurgency doctrine and training. Many of the same criticisms are being leveled today:

The Administration's emphasis on developing a counterinsurgency capability impacted heavily on the Army brass. They were, in effect, being told to alter radically the Army's method of operation, method that had been eminently successful in prior conflicts. The notion that a group of novice civilians ([John F.] Kennedy, [Robert S.] McNamara, and the Whiz Kids') should require the Army to deemphasize what had been its strong suit (*i.e., heavy units, massed firepower, high technology) in favor of stripped-down light infantry units encountered strong organizational resistance.*

Statements from the Army's leadership set out both the organization's disinterest in the President's proposals and their conviction that the concept (the conventional approach to war) could handle any problems that might crop up at the lower end of the conflict spectrum:

General Lyman Lemnitzer, Chairman of the JCS [Joint Chiefs of Staff], 1960–1962: stated that the new administration was "oversold" on the importance of guerrilla warfare.

General George Decker, Army Chief of Staff, 1960–1962, countered a presidential lecture to the Chiefs on counterinsurgency with the reply "any good soldier can handle guerrillas."

General Earle Wheeler, Army Chief of Staff, 1962–1964: "*The essence of the problem in Vietnam in military.*"

General Maxwell Taylor, Chairman of the JCS, 1962–1964: recalling his reaction to JFK's proposals: "It (counterinsurgency) is just a form of small war, a guerrilla operation in which we have a long record against the Indians. *Any well-trained organization can shift the tempo to that which might be required in this kind of situation.* All this cloud of dust that's coming out of the White House really isn't necessary."[1]

STILL PREPARING FOR THE WRONG WAR?

The Army's disinterest with regard to the development of counterinsurgency capability was demonstrated not only in that mechanistic approach in which is addressed this requirement in the 1960's, but also in the manner in which once the "aberration" of Vietnam ended, the organization discarded what had always been an unwanted appendage to its concepts.[2]

Given the proposition that low-intensity conflict is our most likely form of involvement in the Third World, it appears that the Army is still preparing for the wrong war by emphasizing the Soviet threat on the plains of Europe (fondly called the "Fulda Gap" mentality). This concern should not preclude preparations to assist our allies in meeting the threat of internal subversion and guerrilla warfare.

The triumph of the *Sandinistas* in Nicaragua, the insurgency in El Salvador and Cuba's renewed efforts in the Caribbean Basin have conspired to force the Army to reevaluate its priorities and, like St. Paul on the road to Damascus, many have become converts and begun to reassess our capability. The USACGSC curriculum is now back to a modest 32 hours, and old counterinsurgency lesson plans are being dusted off at the service schools. And serious work, albeit modest, is beginning in the service schools, staff colleges and senior service schools.

The Special Forces, faced with drastic personnel cuts in 1979, have been resuscitated and are expanding modestly. Somewhat surprisingly, senior naval officers were instrumental in saving the Special Forces as they questioned the diminution of their "unconventional warfare" assets in the Pacific and Caribbean regions. The 8th Special Action Force (SAF) for Latin America was deactivated in 1973, and the Latin American counterinsurgency capability was reduced to a single Special Forces battalion at Fort Gulick, Panama. The 7th Special Forces Group (Airborne) at Fort Bragg, North Carolina, is now oriented toward the region and presently provides the bulk of the training assistance for Honduras and El Salvador. Apparently, the nadir of our Special Forces capability has been reached and is being expanded slightly to meet the new challenge of the 1980s and 1990s.

What concerns many of us is that these welcome changes stop far short of a serious commitment by the services to devote the personnel and curriculum hours that are needed for adequate instruction *throughout the various educational systems*—the place where long-term changes are made. Thirty-two hours at the Army's mid-level staff college hardly constitute a renaissance for low-intensity conflict. And a few hours of counterinsurgency-related tactical training do not adequately prepare our junior officers for this most likely arena.

Nor are the other services any better prepared than the Army. The Air Force devoted 20 hours to low-intensity conflict and counterinsurgency at the Air Command and Staff College, Maxwell Air Force Base, Alabama, (up to about 50 hours by 1986) and there are no units today with the training and capabilities that would be equivalent to those of the Air Commandos of the 1960s. The Navy and the Air Force still do not have foreign area officer programs that adequately prepare officers for duty in advisory or training assistance roles. The Air Force officers sent to El Salvador during my tenure there were fine pilots and administrators. However, they were totally lacking in language qualification and regional preparation, not to mention the unique aspects of insurgency and counterinsurgency.

Fortunately, the Navy was able to find two superb sea-air-land team (SEAL) officers for duty in El Salvador, but the personnel managers constantly attempted to push "blue water" conventional sailors into what was essentially a brown water, low-intensity conflict situation. All of the services are having difficulty providing counterinsurgency-trained, area-oriented, and language-qualified senior officers for El Salvador. The psychological operations and civil affairs capabilities needed to support our advisory effort in Central America is inadequate. It may be that the U.S. defense establishment is still wary of becoming involved in another Vietnam.

I recently heard two comments from more conventionally oriented colleagues: "Who gives a damn about a bunch of chili-dip countries?" and "It smells like Nuc-Mam to me." While these comments may not reflect Department of Defense policy, they do portray some traditionalists' indifferent and "gun-shy" attitudes toward small wars that we are unprepared to fight.

Given today's realities, however, failure to adequately prepare for low-intensity conflict is inexcusable. I remember the attitude of the Army personnel "wallahs" early in the 1960s. They did everything they could to discourage combat arms officers from serving at the Vietnamese unit and subsector levels. "What you need is troop duty in Europe with a 'Regular' (for example, conventional) unit." After U.S. troop units were committed to Vietnam, duty with the Military Assistance Command, Vietnam, was still considered to be less "career-enhancing" than duty with a U.S. unit. Despite the lessons of post-World War II insurgencies and the experiences of officers, such as Generals William B. Rosson, Edward Lansdale, or John K. Singlaub, we are essentially where we were when Kennedy became president.

Our track record in dealing with insurgencies in Latin America may account, in part, for our present indifference. In the 1960s, with our help, most guerrilla movements in the region were effectively neutralized by Latin-American armies. In 1964, the peak year of the mobile training team effort, we provided 275 of these teams from the 8th SAF in Panama alone. By 1970, the number was down to 70, and most of those were technical assistance teams of one or two specialists each. Our Latin-American allies had by then established their own training centers and cadres, and they were capable of putting rural guerrillas and urban-based terrorists supported by Fidel Castro out of business. In 1967, for example, a 15-member Special Forces mobile training team trained the Bolivian Rangers that made short work of Ernesto "Che" Guevara's adventure. By the late 1960s, it appeared that Castro would have to look elsewhere for excitement.

Nicaragua (1979) changed all that. The Marxist-Leninists used a popularly based insurgency to achieve power. Castro has finally convinced Moscow that revolution in Central America is possible without waiting for *all* objective conditions to exist. The changed role of the Latin American church since the Medellin (Columbia) Conference (1968) and the subsequent radicalization of some churchmen and women have added a new dimension to insurgency.

Most importantly, the effective orchestration of U.S. public opinion by sympathetic interest and front groups and their impact on congressional security assistance support has given new life to Castro-supported, Marxist-Leninist insurgencies. More sophisticated planning and coordination is evident in El Salvador, in Grenada and throughout the region. While Castro has learned from the mistakes of the 1960s, we still appear to have difficulty recovering from our Vietnam hangover.

A recent book on Central America, *Rift and Revolution: The Central American Imbroglio*, contains a superb chapter on "Revolutionary Movements in Central America" by Ernest Evans. Evans concludes:

> For both doctrinal and organizational reasons revolutionary warfare goes deeply against the grain of the U.S. military. The doctrinal problem is that in the U.S. military there has always been a widely shared belief that military issues are and should be kept separate from political issues. The organizational problem is that the U.S. military is a big-unit, high-technology military. Wars against guerrillas, however, for the most part, require small units and fairly simple technology. Although the U.S. military could, of course, modify its organizational patterns, the war in Vietnam demonstrated that the U.S. military is extremely reluctant to modify its big-unit, high-technology orientation.[3]

The fear of becoming involved in another quagmire is evident everywhere in the Department of Defense and, as a result, we are not adequately prepared for any involvement short of commitment of U.S. combat units. Security, training and advisory assistance are the keys to success in counterinsurgency and, if utilized early enough, will preclude the need for the deployment of U.S. troops in a role for which, given our present conventional preoccupation, we are inadequately trained and doctrinally unsuited. The U.S. counterinsurgency effort, to be effective, must have security, advisory, and training assistance experts who can assess the situation, advise the host country forces on the proper counterinsurgency techniques and training, and equip those forces to do the job. They must be supported by theater and unified command staff officers who understand that counterinsurgency is not just the application of high technology and more logistics, firepower, and mobility.

In many respects, real counterinsurgency techniques are a step toward the primitive (for example, *less* firepower that is more surgically applied). The keys to popular support, the *sine qua non* in counterinsurgency, include psychological operations, civic action, and grass roots, human intelligence work, all of which runs counter to the conventional U.S. concept of war. To be effective in our advice, we should be sending our best trained counterinsurgency experts to assist our allies. We should not, as has generally been the case, send conventionally oriented officers to create a miniature U.S. defense establishment.

Snarled security assistance legislation, arbitrary restrictions on numbers of trainers (for example, a 55-member level in El Salvador), constraints on the trainers' in-country activities (terms of reference), as well as a lack of emphasis in the Army's educational system, and a paucity of fully qualified officers in the services, all indicate that we still have a long way to go to meet the challenge.

PROPOSALS FOR THE FUTURE

Having outlined the problems with low-intensity conflict doctrine, let me turn to some proposed solutions. Our counterinsurgency posture is, as has been outlined, in pretty bad shape. There are, however, some recent positive signs.

The emergence of democratically inspired, antitotalitarian insurgencies around the world (i.e., Nicaragua, Afghanistan, Angola . . .) is an unprecedented phenomenon in international affairs. United States support of these insurgencies as well as our willingness to more actively promote orderly transitions to democracy (Philippines, Haiti), marks a new era of U.S. activism. As President Reagan indicated in his 1983 budget message, "Our foreign policy is oriented to maintaining peace through military strength and diplomatic negotiation."[4] The thrust of recent events, culminating in the punitive raid on Libya in April 1986 leads me to reflect upon the military strength at both ends of the spectrum that must be available to us as we push diplomatic initiatives.

To be sure, the insurgency challenge to this country and our allies is present and clear, requiring measures equal to the task. I propose to examine briefly the areas of analysis, doctrine, organization, and professional military education available to meet that challenge.

Analysis

At the risk of stating the obvious, the insurgency challenge of the 1980s is hardly exclusively military. Economic inequities, social and ethnic tensions, and political imbalances are *many times more important* in creating and sustaining insurgencies than the simple fact of the existence of standing guerrilla forces. Valid insights into the causes of a particular movement are had only by profound analysis of economic, political, social, and religious factors that bind and divide a nation. A purely military staff estimate is inadequate. What is required are in-depth country or regional examinations. Recently published studies indicate the feasibility and utility of such an effort. For example, the Caribbean Basin initiative grew out of one such study conducted under the chairmanship of Henry Kissinger, former National Security Advisor and Secretary of State. The recommendations of the Kissinger Commission, as it has come to be known, are a useful example of the application of this kind of analysis. A Presidential directive brings together experts from diverse fields to create a useful planning document for a specific requirement. The military services, singly or together, are capable of generating such studies for any selected area. But in order to create all-source estimates at the *inter-departmental* level, the National Security Council should issue directives transcending organizational boundaries. The result would be a better product. Upon completion, the recommendations would then be submitted to the executive agent for review and implementation.

Doctrine

Recent experience, unfortunately, indicates that the predisposition of our military representatives will be towards higher technology, more complex logistics, and greater firepower (rather than surgical use of less heavy firepower). Their cultural awareness and linguistic ability may be less than the job requires, and they may have relatively short time horizons. While none of these characteristics are necessarily disqualifying flaws, U.S. culture and national experience are very powerful conditioning factors in the performance of our military advisors. At the outset, they must be trained in the use of, and be adept at, Psychological Operations, Civil Affairs, and Human Intelligence collection.

U.S. advisors are often unprepared to prod host government counterparts into these traditionally "nonmilitary" or "nonlethal" tools of war. First, we need to train ourselves. Only then we can "advise" our counterparts on the really key terrain—the four inches between the ears of the target audience. The subtle interaction of cultural forces within the country are lost to someone flying in a helicopter or driving by in an armored vehicle.

Our counterinsurgency doctrine must include all of the above considerations, be tailored to the region, and inculcate a *long-term view* of problems and their solutions. We all need to look past the next budget cycle, and frame policies for the long haul and protracted periods of conflict. "Winning the war on my watch" should be abhorred. We must also encourage foreign-language proficiency in all the military services. The ability to communicate across cultural and language barriers is essential to the implementation of any approved U.S. policy and any successful counterinsurgency or low-intensity conflict effort.

Military doctrine must also emphasize the interagency nature of our foreign policy efforts. There has developed over the last 20 years an insular attitude by some participants in the policy process. The military requirements seem so urgent that the uniformed services become zealous in conducting their portion of the policy to the exclusion of the essential coordination and consultative process. Coordination is essential. This is particularly true when economic and political issues are paramount, as would be the case, for example, during high urban unemployment or during an election campaign. At such times, the military effort needs to be headed toward the goal of the more critical requirement: nonmilitary objectives. Constant reminders of the often tertiary importance of military support are needed throughout the campaign. Additionally, the U.S. military should become much more involved in the nation-building aspects of counterinsurgency.

Since most insurgency movements are found in preindustrial societies, the doctrine should include low-technology responses. Computers, laser range finders, and jet fighters do not lead the assisted country's military to critical thinking about the causes, and the cures, of the problems they face. Acquisition of high technology in place of boots, adequate field rations, eyeglasses, functional radios, or reliable individual weapons is an error we seem to make with painful regularity. We must pose the question, "What will the acquisition of this piece of equipment do for the individual fighting man as he performs his daily mission?" In no case should equipment be provided whose only function is to occupy space in a warehouse for five years, and for which no operators are available. Acquisition of high technology by the host country should occur only *after the requirements for basic equipment* have been filled, and the host country's infrastructure can manage and maintain it. Weapons systems should focus on the threat, keeping the level of violence down, and minimizing collateral damage. When I was the Military Group Commander in El Salvador, I fought a constant battle to keep technology at the lowest levels and stressed people-intensive, low-technology options. High-performance aircraft, while viable in the medium- to high-intensity conflict arenas, are least suited for counterinsurgency since they are unable to separate the insurgents from the general population. *U.S. military doctrine should force our hosts to think small and develop remedies that treat the causes of insurgency rather than its symptoms.*

Organization

The organization to support such a counterinsurgency/low-intensity conflict policy should incorporate all aspects of analysis and doctrine previously addressed. Within the Unified Commands, the establishment of Special Operations Commands (SOCs) provides a Joint Command and Control capability, staffed and organized to implement approved policy. The SOC, as a sub-Unified Command within the theater, acts as the Commander in Chief's executive agent for planning and conducting assistance training and advisory missions within the context of preparing for theater-wide, approved contingency plans. A possible scenario for SOC employment of assets would be the provision of a Mobile Training Team (MTT) to train within a designated country faced with the early stages of insurgency. This training would be followed by small, intense field exercises planned by some of the same advisors who participated in the original MTT. The scenario for the exercise would serve to evaluate the MTTs' training and reveal weakness and other training requirements for the future. These MTT exercises, and the resulting after-action reports, would be provided to the U.S. country team and regional planning group for interagency study. As interagency planning continues, future policy objectives would be provided to the SOC Commander and his staff for their study and implementation as required.

Within the U.S. Army, the focal points for counterinsurgency and LIC policy execution are the Special Forces Groups, the Rangers, and the Light Infantry Divisions. These organizations should be regionally oriented and provide current expertise on doctrine and tactics suited to the situation in the region. These units should train with the country forces and conduct continuous exchanges of individuals and units in order to upgrade training and interoperability techniques. Deployment of these forces in contingency operations will be at the request of the supported commander in chief and deftly planned to fulfill the requirements of a coordinated policy position. As the commander revises his force requirements for military activity in theater, the SOC, as a sub-Unified Command, receives operational command of forces to conduct operations at the low end of the spectrum of conflict. Since the spectrum includes all insurgent activities, the SOC will frame Army requirements to utilize the capabilities of Special Forces Groups, Rangers, and Light Infantry Divisions. This may require simultaneous deployments of Light Infantry Forces and/or Rangers on an exercise, while Special Forces are conducting security assistance and training activities. This entire operation would be under the command of the SOC or a designated Joint Task Force in the country. The orchestration of supporting Civil Affairs, Psychological Operations and Human Intelligence activities would come under the SOC, but could be delegated to the Special Forces commander on site. The final "fix" should include a Security Assistance Force with all these elements under a single commander, who is forward deployed in the theater.

Professional Military Education

Changing the underlying structure of counterinsurgency and low-intensity conflict (COIN/LIC) doctrine and organization requires changes in the professional education provided to our officers and noncommissioned officers in three key areas:

1. low-intensity conflict study
2. joint operations exercises
3. language and cultural training

Low-intensity conflict should be studied at *all* levels of the U.S. professional military education system. The case study method is very useful. Recent experiences in El Salvador, Honduras, Afghanistan, Angola, Guatemala, Chad,

Lebanon, Cambodia, provide excellent foundations for case studies. Lectures by people with recent experience in this kind of work offer good opportunities for critical thought. Study of interviews with Marxist-Leninist insurgents also will pay off. Some progress in the military's school systems is evident. The general tendency, however, is toward focusing on terrorism rather than on the foundation and dynamics of revolutions and low-intensity conflict.

Recent congressional initiatives to reform the Joint Chiefs of Staff emphasize the future of military operations worldwide. And, in February 1987, the Pentagon proposed to Congress a new special operations command to combat terrorism and engage in low-intensity conflict, that would group Army, Navy, and Air Force elements under a high-level civilian deputy and a four-star general.[5] Joint operations planning and execution will be the key to the success of our future low-intensity conflict policies. The process of planning and executing counter-insurgency must include all services and non-Department of Defense. The military education system, particularly for the field grades, must emphasize the Joint aspect. The Joint arena requires an understanding of each service and this education should be a part of each service's education system. The military education system must continue to contribute in a major way to low-intensity conflict.

The challenge of language and culture present a formidable obstacle to many of our military personnel. Often an American, choosing the military service as a career, has made a subliminal commitment to the essential rightness of U.S. policy and interests. This, at times, unquestioning faith in all things American can sometimes limit perception of tradeoffs necessary to advance the overall purpose of a particular policy. The example of U.S. military advisors who press the host country to adopt a professional NCO cadre ignores the cultural, societal, and economic impediments to what is essentially a host country's leadership problem.

The ability to speak the language and the opportunity that ability provides for gaining information is a paramount attribute. The military assignment process should include formal training in language *before* the service member is assigned to the country. When these training opportunities have been provided, we have seen improved operational compatibility between parts, units, people, and unit efficiency. Another possible answer to improving the communications capability is the assignment or attachment of capable allied nationals to U.S. units and to U.S. military schools. This policy works well in Korea and would be useful in other situations as well. Without question, these host country nationals with U.S. unit experience are better emissaries from their own culture and society, capable of representing the requirements and policies of their own government to us.

None of the above proposals alone will satisfy all requirements for the kind of military strength needed to back up our diplomatic initiatives in counterinsurgency and low-intensity conflict. However, we need to make a strong beginning. The purpose of our military is to defend the nation. That defense, to be effective in LIC, as with the conventional, mid-, or high-intensity conflict, must be practiced in advance and requires novel thinking and much more responsive institutions. If we cannot meet the LIC challenge well forward, then maybe we should think about digging in along the Mexican border.

ACKNOWLEDGMENT

The first half of this essay draws on Colonel Waghelstein's ''Post-Vietnam Counterinsurgency Doctrine,'' *Military Review*, Vol. LXV, No. 5, May 1985, pp. 42–49. Reprinted with permission of *Military Review*.

NOTES

1. Andrew F. Krepinevitch, *The United States Army in Vietnam: Counterinsurgency Doctrine and the Army Concept of War*, Study, (U.S. Military Academy, West Point, N.Y.), pp. 25–26. (Emphasis added).

2. Ibid., p. 71. (Emphasis added).

3. *Rift and Revolution: The Central American Imbroglio*, edited by Howard J. Wiarda (American Enterprise Institute for Public Policy Research, Washington, D.C., 1984), pp. 186–87.

4. President Ronald Reagan to Congress, January 31, 1983.

5. James M. Dorsey, ''Pentagon to push new plan for anti-terrorism command,'' *Washington Times* (3 February, 1987), p. 3.

Lessons, Legacies, and Implications of Vietnam

Interest in the American war in Vietnam has increased dramatically in recent years. After a decade of a post-war, intellectual dark age, interest in that most difficult of conflicts has spawned considerable new research, writing, and discussion. Nowhere is this more evident than on the college campuses, where classes on the Vietnam War are often standing room only by a post-Vietnam generation of students thirsting for knowledge about the war. It is still difficult to be truly objective about the Vietnam War. On the one hand, we have the "hawks" who thought that an all-out military effort could have decisively defeated the Vietnamese communists in a shorter time. On the other hand, the "doves" saw the war as either too complex, or unwinnable, or not worth the cost.

In retrospect, the war's complexities bar the rendering of simple judgments— but some qualified judgments can be offered. It is clear that the United States misunderstood the character and history of the Vietnamese people, and underestimated both the political fragmentation in the South and the will and the staying power of the regime in the North. Perhaps Americans were victims of their own capabilities. After all, no less than General of the Army George C. Marshall averred that Americans were not able to fight a long war.

Moreover, nations usually fight when vital interests are involved, but there was no American consensus that vital interests were at stake in Vietnam. Would the war have been fought differently if U.S. vital interests had been at stake? Further, the United States brought high-technology, conventional military forces into a low-technology, heavily political and, at least partly, unconventional environment. Could the elephant ever have cornered the cheetah? Despite near total mechanization of U.S. and allied infantry (to include "air mobile" brigades), the communists were fundamentally the more mobile force, unrestricted by the lack of good roads, or good weather, or thousands of allied fire bases. They held the initiative. They controlled the tempo of the war.

And, of course, there was the impact of television and other forms of media on this war and its outcome. Vietnam was the first major war in history to be televised, or rather to be televised to *one* side. One is reminded of George Will's observation that if television cameras had been at Gettysburg, the United States would be two countries today.

Having placed the war in brief perspective, important themes and areas of disagreement appear in the essays in this book, and they reflect issues that were evident among U.S. officers and officials charged with conducting the American war in Vietnam. These problems are discussed in the following sections:

THE NATURE OF THE WAR

Was Vietnam a *conventional* war whose source or origin was North Vietnam (Harry Summers and Alan Gropman), or a *revolutionary* war in which the Viet Cong had a relatively independent role, at least until Tet 1968 (Lawrence Grinter, Nguyen Hung, Peter Dunn, Noel Eggleston, and Earl Tilford)? Moreover, was the war in Vietnam primarily *military*, or *political*, or both? General Earle Wheeler, the U.S. Army Chief of Staff during 1962–1964, stated: "The essence of the problem in Vietnam is military." But Douglas Pike, the American authority on Vietnamese communism, argued that the war was a political struggle with violent military overtones; "an ultra hostile bloodletting" with basic "non-military" aspects.

Those are fundamentally different views, and U.S. conduct in Vietnam never reconciled that basic split. It is interesting that most (although not all) U.S. military officers saw Vietnam as a conventional war, while most civilian officials (again not all) viewed the war as a revolutionary contest in which the heart of the problem lay in South Vietnam, not North Vietnam. What produced this debilitating disagreement? The most immediate explanation is differences in training, and differences in bureaucratic loyalties. Almost all U.S. military officers are trained for conventional war, not unconventional war, and they make their careers preparing for and managing conventional military contingencies. By contrast the senior civilians involved in the Vietnam War tended to have a wider range of backgrounds and education. They were more sensitive to political, social, and psychological aspects of the war.

U.S. military officers and civilian officials carried these differences into the war, *and the affect on strategy was devastating*. The old bureaucratic adage that "where you stand depends on when you sit" played itself out in Vietnam. American military and civilian leaders did not heed the Clausewitzian admonition that "the first, the supreme, the most far-reaching act of judgment that the statesman and commander have to make is to establish . . . the kind of war on which they are embarking." We know of little in the post-Vietnam atmosphere that has corrected, or even fundamentally addressed, this split between military and civilian perceptions about low-intensity conflicts. The incentives within the

U.S. military are still toward careerism based on conventional, high-technology conflicts, with a European focus.

BUREAUCRATIC FRAGMENTATION

Coordination between the U.S. armed forces and between U.S. military and civilian agencies in Vietnam was very poor. The Army and Marines had different ideas about how the ground war and pacification should be waged and there were significant squabbles within the Army itself. The ''Regular'' Army fought a separate war from the unconventional soldiers (the Special Forces), and their antagonism grew to the extent that the Special Forces were packed up and sent home in 1971. The Air Force controlled only a portion of the bombing in Indochina, because the Navy and Marines would not submit to Air Force operational control. Within the Air Force, the Strategic Air Command would not relinquish control of its forces to the 7th Air Force Commander in Vietnam. Add to this situation a number of civilian agencies, including the State Department, the Central Intelligence Agency, the Agency for International Development, and more—each with its own lines of communication to its Washington headquarters and to Congress—and the United States created an almost unmanageable situation. Feeble attempts to bring it all under control of the Country Team failed. There was no single manager control. ''Bureaucracy,'' as Robert Komer observed, ''did its thing.''

More recent instances of multiservice operations—the Iranian rescue mission, the Grenada invasion, and the Libyan air strikes—indicate that bureaucratic fragmentation still bedevils U.S. performance. All military services were written into the Iranian plan, with the result being that no overall joint proposals were implemented and that logistics and training problems (which proved fatal) were not anticipated. The Grenada invasion plan, rightly the purview of the Commander in Chief, Atlantic, was rewritten to include the Army (to justify use of Rangers) and the Air Force (jealous of leaving everything to the Navy and Marines). The resulting operational problems make one shudder to think what could have happened had a stronger opponent (like Nicaragua) been on the field. The U.S. air attacks on Libya in April 1986 reflected turf problems between the Air Force (and its units based in Great Britain) and the Navy's assets right off Libya's shores.

In Vietnam, perhaps more competent commanders could have pulled it all together, as did, for example, General Sir Gerald Templar in Malaya in a much smaller conflict. But Templar was also the High Commissioner (ambassador), and thus held wider powers; he was, in effect, London's proconsul. Yet no less than General Maxwell Taylor compromised this option in Vietnam by declining President Johnson's offer to invest his position as the American Ambassador with very strong powers and to place all resources under single manager control. The communists, by contrast, never made that mistake.

ALTERNATIVE STRATEGIES

Were there alternatives to U.S./GVN strategy in Vietnam? Many schools of thought contend, and they even disagree, as well, on the strategy that *was actually* used in the Vietnam War. Harry Summers argues that U.S. strategy concentrated on the wrong target—counterinsurgency against the Viet Cong rather than conventional operations against North Vietnam. Summers believes that insurgency in South Vietnam was a deliberate NVA "smoke screen." But Nguyen Hung demonstrates that internal Vietnamese disagreements within the South as well as between southerners and northerners played a role. And Lawrence Grinter argues that for all the *rhetoric* placed on counterinsurgency and pacification, the *actual resources* devoted to it were miniscule compared to the conventional resources applied in both South Vietnam and against North Vietnam. Summers wanted to strike the North Vietnamese "center of gravity" with a military invasion of the DRV. But Noel Eggleston underlines the reasons for President Johnson's deliberate limiting of the U.S. role in Vietnam. And Peter Dunn, Lawrence Grinter, and Noel Eggleston are skeptical that an invasion, if ordered, could have succeeded, given NVA tenacity, ARVN incompetence, and the probability that China would have intervened on North Vietnam's behalf. Alan Gropman argues that U.S. air power should have been unleashed early in the war to compel the DRV to lay off South Vietnam. (One is reminded of General LeMay's reported statement: "Its time to stop swatting flies and instead hit the manure pile.") But Earl Tilford is skeptical that such an all-out attack could have been successful, citing the overconfidence of U.S. air power enthusiasts, the probability that the Viet Cong would have fought on, and other political-military constraints on a *Linebacker I* or *II*-type operation in 1965–1966.

Whereas Summers and Gropman wanted *more* American military power applied, Hung and Grinter pointed out the effects on South Vietnam of the power that *was* applied: the corruption and black marketeering, the refugee generation, and the enormous social dislocation—all disruptive of strategy. In short, there is little agreement on alternative strategies.

U.S. PREPARATION FOR FUTURE WARS

If training and loyalties were so devastating on the design and conduct of U.S. strategy in Vietnam, and if there were such strong disagreements on the causes for the violence in South Vietnam, what prospects are there for more agreement among military and civilian professionals in the future? They are not promising. Shortly after the United States terminated its Vietnam involvement, U.S. professional military education (PME) almost completely dropped topics dealing with revolutionary war, counterinsurgency, and internal defense and development. As John Waghelstein points out, the Army (and the Air Force) saw Vietnam as an "aberration" from their need to stay prepared for the Soviet threat on the plains of Europe. Indeed in the late 1970s and early 1980s, the

Vietnam War was *not even mentioned* in FM–100–5, the Army's most important operations manual.

However, in the decade after the fall of Saigon, low-intensity conflict, internal subversion, and guerrilla wars have laid siege to the Third World with critical losses to United States and allied interests. Vietnam, Cambodia, Laos, Angola, Mozambique, Yemen, Afghanistan are a few examples and they testify to the fact that the most likely form of future conflict—the one which U.S. armed services are least prepared for—has already arrived. Preparation for low-intensity conflict should be integrated into *all* levels of the U.S. military system, educationally, organizationally, and in terms of careers. But, to date, PME curricula shows only a grudging acceptance of this kind of material—about 40 to 50 hours at the command and staff colleges, less at the senior service schools.

In the field, advisors working in low-intensity conflict environments should resist incentives toward high technology, complex logistics, and greater firepower. They should be educated in local cultural and political realities, and their careers should receive the same incentives as officers in more conventional military fields and management. Advisors (and the supervisors who put them there) have to understand that nonmilitary factors (host military relations with the people, levels of corruption, inequitable distributions of wealth, lack of jobs) are often *more* important concerns of the civilian population than the guerrilla threat in the countryside. The military's inevitable tendency to attack the symptoms of the conflict rather than its causes is a constant factor which must be understood and controlled.

A FINAL PERSPECTIVE

In looking back on the American war in Vietnam, other problems demonstrated themselves that will undoubtedly affect the United States's next intervention. One problem certainly was our naïveté and overconfidence. The United States assumed that our power and our resources would simply overwhelm our adversaries. We were wrong and we underestimated both their endurance and our impatience. Moreover, politicians accustomed to business in Washington seldom grasped the fact that commitments were measured by different yardsticks in Hanoi, Moscow, and Beijing, where party leaders do not have to play to media, be concerned with short-term gain or reelections, nor are they troubled by organized political opposition or powerful lobbies capable of deflecting government policies. When democracies take on totalitarianisms, the contest, by definition, is unequal. Khe Sanh was a case in point. With the U.S. president fearful of suffering a major loss on the order of the earlier Dien Bien Phu defeat of the French, huge American resources were tied down to protect the remote camp and airstrip, in which two U.S. Marine regiments were encircled so tightly that they could not even perform that most basic of infantry operations, the patrol. American leaders evidently thought that General Vo Nguyen Giap would repeat his tactics of 1954, thus allowing superior American firepower to be brought to bear on the elusive enemy. The only similarity between Dien Bien Phu and Khe Sanh was the search by the Western powers for the decisive set-piece battle. In both cases that battle came, and in both cases it was a turning point of the war. In 1968, American media-prompted obsession with that encircled camp helped the communists slip large numbers of troops into position elsewhere in South Vietnam to execute the Tet offensive. The resultant political shock in the West (again via television) was the beginning of the end for America in Vietnam. Few senior American military or civilian leaders seemed able to comprehend the communist strategy at the time. It may simply be that the American philosophy that "the future is now," on which U.S. politicians both in and out of uniform are raised, prohibits development of the kind of intellectual and conceptual depth needed to understand and meet these challenges. If simple superiority in technology and firepower was the answer, the war would have been no contest. But there was more to it, much more.

Much Western criticism was aimed at our ally, the South Vietnamese, who were said to be venal, corrupt, poor soldiers, and so on. Yet the South Vietnamese fought bravely and, when populations and casualties are compared, took on the order of *60 times* more casualties than the United States! Moreover, it might be argued that there was more corruption in Washington than in Saigon. In recent years, for example, hundreds of U.S. officials have been charged with corruption, scores convicted, and these ranged from the President's cabinet on down. In South Vietnam, a U.S. infantry private's pay was more than that of an ARVN Colonel's pay. So perhaps we should not focus too closely on the corruption issue.

More serious was the incessant hammering of the Government of South Vietnam on "human rights," from the mauling taken by the Diem government over the handling of the Buddhist riots to Thieu's "tiger cages." American media, once they get their backs up, do not show a pronounced tolerance about other cultures' ways of doing things. And of course without access to North Vietnam's prisons, American media had nothing to say at all about the DRV's atrocious human rights practices. One U.S. Ambassador to Saigon, Frederick Nolting, was appalled at the American treatment of Diem and his government, and to this day lays responsibility for the downfall of Diem and the ultimate unraveling of the South Vietnamese political structure to U.S. administrations that bent with every wind and American media that were interested in making mischief and money. Minor South Vietnamese excesses stirred a liberal Western press to a much greater degree than did worse communist crimes against humanity. How would the media have treated the GVN had its cadres massacred 3,000 city leaders and dumped them into mass graves, as did the communists in 1968 in Hue? Yet, ironically, political disturbances arose in the South precisely because there was *more* freedom, and *less* governmental control, than in the North. Thus, the Buddhists, the Cao Dai, the Hoa Hao, and others could demonstrate, riot, and run their own affairs to a significant degree *because* South Vietnam's governments did not exercise the kind of totalitarianism extant in North Vietnam.

Americans sympathetic to the communists went to Hanoi and supported that grim totalitarian regime. There is hardly any scholar of significance who does not ascribe a share of blame for the fall of South Vietnam to the American news media, yet few significant studies have been made of this phenomenon.

Another curious aspect of the American war in Vietnam is that with the exception of a few official or quasi-official studies, it was largely put into the closet. Unlike most Western nations, the United States conducted no official inquiry into the failure. This is not to say that academics and individuals are ignoring the subject—quite the contrary is true. But no governing American administration ordered a thorough look into the political and military conduct of the war. In fact, in numerous instances, one or more of the military services have denied officers permission to write unclassified scholarly articles about the war—which by American standards is now almost ancient history. This situation is changing, but only gradually.

Then there was, and continues to be, the U.S. managerial mindset as a substitute for strategic thinking. United States military officers are relative amateurs, not professionals, in the disciplines of strategy, history, geopolitics, and even leadership (which is increasingly equated in the military to "management"). Reasons are evident: too little time on the job and too few career incentives. The average officer spends just three or four years in the field, then goes to a school or staff job. He stays in the staff job for three or four years, in an 8-to-5, businesslike job, then goes back to the field again—where he must polish his rusty operational proficiency. After three or four years in the field, he's off again, back to another school or desk, and after about fifteen years, he's usually deskbound until he retires. Thus the armed forces have a continual revolving door that swings generalists and specialists in and out of operational jobs punctuated by schools increasingly devoted to technical and managerial topics. History, politics, culture and languages fall by the wayside.

The study of history would have little value unless something is learned and used from it. History is particularly appropriate to the lessons of conflict in Vietnam, where earlier Vietnamese heroes, bereft of high-powered universities and high-technology computers, knew very well how their earlier military commanders had fought and won against more powerful foreign enemies. When the great Tran Hung Dao impaled the Chinese river fleet on iron spikes, then destroyed their army in a fearful massacre, he was repeating the tactics that had been used more than three hundred years earlier (in the same place) by Ngo Quyen. The Vietnamese have for centuries relied on what is now called "low-intensity conflict," guerrilla warfare, insurgency, and revolutionary war, to harry and wear out enemies whose military strength was greater than their own. The Vietnamese glorified their own military history and were intimately familiar with the fact that their earlier commanders had succeeded repeatedly in combining terrain, weather, strategy, tactics, and determination against formidable foes. By contrast U.S. officials and military forces knew little about irregular warfare— which for them was, in effect, anything that differed from the European central front or the Korean War models, and they knew practically nothing about their Vietnamese enemies or allies.

The Vietnam War exhibited the almost instinctive American reliance on the high-technology fix. But addictions can be both costly and, in the withdrawal stages, painful. The rush to computerize all aspects of the war cost the American effort in numerous ways—both conceptually and operationally. For example, the Hamlet Evaluation System in the pacification effort emphasized *resources pumped into hamlets* rather than the Vietnamese peoples actual allegiances and behavior. Measures of effort were substituted for effectiveness. In the air war over North Vietnam, operations had to be halted for several days when the 7th Air Force's main computer broke down. Since no orders, rules of engagement or targets could be manually transmitted to the operational air wings, the air war simply stopped. The implications of these technology imperatives are potentially frightening, for they render the United States not only vulnerable to wartime paralysis, but increasingly irrelevant in its thinking.

In Vietnam, the enormous military support establishment, the "tooth to tail ratio," caused by the growing sophistication and dependency of the U.S. armed forces, resulted in the creation of huge base areas with hundreds of thousands of young soldiers with time on their hands after working hours. The impact on Vietnamese society of these large numbers of well-paid, high-spending, ignorant foreigners was extraordinary; a smaller number later helped to produce the sort of revulsion which, in Iran, brought an anti-Western religious despot to power. How much this U.S. impact contributed to the destruction of South Vietnam's social fabric has yet to be fully understood, but its effect was probably measurable. Finally breakdowns in discipline and moral fiber saw instances of American soldiers murdering their own officers and NCOs in alarming numbers—the term was called "fragging"—using fragmentation grenades.

The relative conventional military weakness of the United States in relation to the Soviet Union was highlighted by the Vietnam War. If this was the "half war" of the "one-and-a-half war" strategy for which the U.S. military forces were sized to fight, then clearly a simultaneous conflict in Europe would have had disastrous consequences. One wonders how another major war could have been managed. For example, U.S. units in Europe often become dangerously (under strength) because of the demands of the war in Southeast Asia. Thus, in 1969 and 1970, one of the editors was assigned to an RF–4C (Phantom) squadron in Europe. The squadron was authorized 26 pilots and 26 Weapons Systems Officers (WSOs), but for long periods had only 13 pilots and 9 WSOs. Since there were no commensurate decreases in operational commitments, the crews flew twice as often as normal; all three of the wing's squadrons were similarly stretched, which contributed to the ever-growing fatigue of the aircrews and eventually to the loss of six aircraft and three lives in fairly rapid succession.

One of the lessons that the Vietnam War should most teach us is that the United States must be able to meet different military challenges in widely differing battlegrounds. *It cannot try to change the war to suit its existing force structure, or doctrine.* Rather, the reverse is true—the forces must be flexible enough to adapt to the conditions at hand. Ironically, the touted "flexible response" was anything but that. *Instead of the response being flexible in the true sense of the term, it was simply smaller or bigger doses of the same response.* The United States cannot count on having Grenadian-sized opponents in the future—nor do operations on that island give us much confidence that the military has really adapted to low-intensity warfare.

The Vietnam War, despite its sad ending, went on long enough to provide plenty of insights on what happened and why the United States failed. This book has examined numerous reasons for the failure, reasons that would again be fatal should the United States become militarily involved with another reasonably strong power in a protracted conflict. It would be gratifying for us to be able to write that the lessons of the failure have been understood—truly probed and understood—and that the nation's defenses and defense establishment have fundamentally profited by such understanding. There have been a few changes. Military reform is in the air. But the evidence does not suggest that the United States is now capable of fighting difficult, irregular wars against determined enemies. Our country has trouble even dealing with drug smuggling across its own borders (fragmentation of effort, turf battles, and corruption all apply). F–15 and F–16 jets, naval cruisers, and Abrams tanks will be next to useless in low-intensity conflicts. While the next U.S. major military involvement undoubtedly will be in a Third World region, our forces remain structured almost exclusively for the war that will not be. Low-intensity conflict, the offspring of the Vietnam War, seems hardly more understood by U.S. officials, military or civilian, than the American war in Vietnam.

Selected Bibliography

Alger, John I. *The Quest for Victory*. Westport, Conn.: Greenwood Press, 1982.

Armitage, M. J., and R. A. Mason. *Air Power in the Nuclear Age*. Chicago: University of Illinois Press, 1983.

Baritz, Loren. *Backfire: American Culture and the Vietnam War*. New York: Ballantine Books, 1985.

Berger, Carl, editor. *The United States Air Force in Southeast Asia, 1961–1973: An Illustrated Account*, rev. ed. Washington, D.C.: Office of Air Force History, 1984.

Berman, Larry. *Planning a Tragedy*. New York: W. W. Norton & Company, 1982.

Blaufarb, Douglas S. *The Counterinsurgency Era: U.S. Doctrine and Performance, 1950 to the Present*. New York: Free Press, 1977.

Braestrup, Peter, editor. *Vietnam as History Ten Years After the Paris Peace Accords*. Washington, D.C.: University Press of America, 1984.

Buttinger, Joseph. *Vietnam: The Unforgettable Tragedy*. New York: Horizon Press, 1977.

———. *The Smaller Dragon: A Political History of Vietnam*. New York: Praeger, 1958.

Clausewitz, Karl von. *On War*. Edited and translated by Michael Howard, and Peter Paret. Princeton, N.J.: Princeton University Press, 1976.

Corson, William. *The Betrayal*. New York: W. W. Norton, 1968.

———. *Consequences of Failure*. New York: W. W. Norton & Company, 1974.

Crithfield, Richard. *The Long Charade: Political Subversion in the Vietnam War*. New York: Harcourt, Brace and World, 1966.

Currey, Cecil B. *Self-Destruction: The Disintegration and Decay of the United States Army During the Vietnam Era*. New York: W. W. Norton and Company, 1981.

Dinh, Nguyen Thi. *No Other Roads to Take: Memoir of Mrs. Nguyen Thi Dinh*. Ithaca, N.Y.: Southeast Asia Program, Department of Asian Studies, Cornell University, 1976.

Doglione, John A. et al. *Airpower and the 1972 Spring Invasion*, USAF Southeast Asia Monograph Series. Washington, D.C.: U.S. Government Printing Office, 1976.

Don, Tran Van. *Our Endless War: Inside Vietnam*. San Raphael, Cal.: Presidio Press, 1979.

Doyle, Edward, and Samuel Lipsman, eds. *The Vietnam Experience*. 18 volumes. Vol. 4, *America Takes Over*. Boston: Boston Publishing Company, 1982.

Drew, Dennis M. *Rolling Thunder, 1965: Anatomy of a Failure*. Airpower Research Institute Report No. AU-ARI-CP–86–3. Maxwell AFB, Ala.: Air University Press, 1986.

Duiker, William J. *The Communist Road to Power in Vietnam*. Boulder, Colo.: Westview Press, 1981.

Dung, Van Tien. *Our Great Spring Victory: An Account of the Liberation of South Vietnam*. New York and London: Monthly Review Press, 1977.

Dunn, Peter, "The American Army: The Vietnam War, 1965–1973." *Armed Forces and Modern Counterinsurgency*. Edited by Ian Beckett and John Pimlott. London: Croom, Helm, 1985.

Eckstein, Harry, ed. *Internal War: Problems and Approaches*. New York: Free Press, 1964.

Fall, Bernard B. *The Two Viet-Nams: A Political and Military Analysis*. 2d revised edition. New York: Praeger, 1967.

———. *Street Without Joy: Indochina at War, 1946–54*. Harrisburg, Pa.: Stackpole, 1964.

FitzGerald, Frances. *Fire in the Lake*. New York: Vintage Books, 1973.

Futrell, Robert F. *The United States Air Force in Southeast Asia: The Advisory Years to 1965*. Washington: The Office of Air Force History, 1983.

Gallucci, Robert L. *Neither War Nor Peace: The Politics of American Military Policy in Vietnam*. Baltimore: Johns Hopkins University Press, 1975.

Gates, John M., "Vietnam: The Debate Goes On." *Parameters* 14 (Spring 1984).

Gehri, Suzanne Budd (Major). *Study War Once More: Teaching Vietnam at Air University*. Maxwell AFB, Ala.: Center for Aerospace Doctrine, Research, and Education, 1985.

Gelb, Leslie H., and Richard K. Betts. *The Irony of Vietnam: The System Worked*. Washington, D.C.: The Brookings Institution, 1979.

Giap, Vo Nguyen. *The Military Art of Peoples' War*. New York: Monthly Review Press, 1970.

Goodman, Allan E. "South Vietnam and the New Security." *Asian Survey*, (February 1972).

Graebner, Norman A., "American Foreign Policy after Vietnam," *Parameters*, (Autumn 1985).

Grinter, Lawrence E., "Bargaining Between Saigon and Washington: Dilemmas of Linkage Politics During War," *Orbis* 18:3 (Fall 1974).

———. "South Vietnam: Pacification Denied." *South-East Asian SPECTRUM* 3:4 (July 1975).

———. "How They Lost: Doctrines, Strategies and Outcomes of the Vietnam War." *Asian Survey* 15:12 (December 1975).

Haines, David W., ed. *Refugees in the United States*. Westport, Conn.: Greenwood Press, 1985.

Halberstam, David. *The Best and the Brightest*. New York: Random House, 1972.

Hannah, Norman B. "Vietnam, Now We Know." *All Quiet on the Eastern Front*. Edited by Anthony T. Bouscaren. New York: Devin-Adair, 1977.

Herring, George C. *America's Longest War: The United States in Vietnam, 1950–1975*. New York: Random House, 1979.

Herrington, Stuart A. *Silence Was a Weapon: The Vietnam War in the Villages.* Novato, Cal.: Presidio Press, 1982.

Hilsman, Roger. *To Move a Nation: The Politics of Foreign Policy in the Administration of John F. Kennedy.* Garden City, N.Y.: Doubleday, 1967.

Hosmer, Stephen T., Konrad Kellen, and Brian M. Jenkins. *The Fall of South Vietnam.* New York: Crane, Russak, 1980.

Hung, Nguyen P. "Communist Offensive Strategy and the Defense of South Vietnam." *Parameters* (Winter 1984).

Huy, Nguyen Ngoc. *Vietnam Under Communist Rule.* Fairfax, Va.: The Indochina Institute, George Mason University, 1982.

Kahin, George McT., and John W. Lewis. *The United States in Vietnam.* rev. ed. New York: Dial Press, 1969.

Kattenberg, Paul M. "Reflections on Vietnam: Of Revisionism and Lessons Yet to be Learned." *Parameters* 14 (Autumn 1984).

Karnow, Stanley. *Vietnam: A History.* New York: Viking Press, 1983.

Kearns, Doris. *Lyndon Johnson and the American Dream.* New York: Harper and Row, 1976.

Kinnard, Douglas. *The War Managers.* Hanover, N.H.: University Press of New England, 1977.

Kissinger, Henry A. *White House Years.* New York: Little, Brown and Company, 1979.

Komer, Robert W., *Bureaucracy at War: U.S. Performance in the Vietnam Conflict.* Boulder, Colo.: Westview Press, 1986.

———. "Clear, Hold and Rebuilt." *Army* (May 1970).

———. "Pacification: A Look Back and Ahead," *Army* (June 1970).

Krepinevich, Andrew F., Jr. *The Army and Vietnam.* Baltimore: The Johns Hopkins University Press, 1986.

Ky, Nguyen Cao. *How We Lost the Vietnam War.* New York: Stein & Day, 1978.

Lavelle, A. J. C., editor. *Airpower and the Spring Invasion.* Washington, D.C.: U.S. Government Printing Office, 1976.

Lewy, Guenter. *America in Vietnam.* New York: Oxford University Press, 1978.

———. "Some Political-Military Lessons of the Vietnam War." *Parameters* (Spring 1984).

Littauer, Raphael, and Norman Uphoff, editors. *The Air War in Indochina.* Boston: Beacon Press, 1971.

Lomperis, Timothy. *The War Everyone Lost—and Won; America's Intervention in Viet Nam's Twin Struggles.* Baton Rouge: Louisiana State University Press, 1984.

Long, Nguyen, with Harry H. Kendall. *After Saigon Fell: Daily Life under the Vietnamese Communists.* Berkeley, Cal.: Institute of East Asian Studies, University of California, 1982.

McAllister, John T. *The Origins of Revolution.* New York: Alfred Knopf, 1969.

McCarthy, James R., and George B. Allison. *Linebacker II: A View From the Rock.* Vol. VI, No. 8, USAF Southeast Asia Monograph Series. Washington, D.C.: U.S. Government Printing Office, 1979.

McGarvey, Patrick J., editor. *Visions of Victory: Selected Vietnamese Communist Military Writings, 1964–1968.* Stanford, Cal.: Hoover Institution Press, 1969.

MacLear, Michael. *The Ten Thousand Day War, Vietnam: 1945–1975.* New York: St. Martin's Press, 1981.

Mao Tse-tung. *Selected Military Writings of Mao Tse-tung*. (Peking: Foreign Language Press, 1967.)

Michael, Stanley J., Jr. "Vietnam: Failure to Follow the Principles of War." *Marine Corps Gazette* (August 1977).

Momyer, William W. *Air Power in Three Wars*. Washington, D.C.: U.S. Government Printing Office, 1979.

Morris, Stephen. "Vietnam Under Communism." *Commentary* 74:3 (September 1982).

Nixon, Richard. *No More Vietnams*. New York: Arbor House, 1985.

Palmer, Bruce. *The 25-Year War: America's Military Role in Vietnam*. Lexington: University Press of Kentucky, 1984.

Palmer, Dave Richard. *Summons of the Trumpet: U.S.–Vietnam in Perspective*. San Raphael, Cal.: Presidio Press, 1978.

Parks, W. Hays. "Rolling Thunder and the Law of War." *Air University Review*. (January–February 1982).

Pike, Douglas. *Viet Cong*. Cambridge: MIT Press, 1966.

———. *War, Peace, and the Viet Cong*. Cambridge: MIT Press, 1969.

———. *The Viet-Cong Strategy of Terror*. Saigon: U.S. Mission, 1970.

———. *PAVN: People's Army of Vietnam*. Novato, Cal.: Presidio Press, 1986.

Podhoretz, Norman. *Why We Were in Vietnam*. New York: Simon and Schuster, 1982.

Pool, Ithiel de Sola. "Political Alternatives to the Viet Cong." *Asian Survey* 7:8 (August 1967).

Popkin, Samuel L. "Colonialism and the Ideological Origins of the Vietnamese Revolution." *Journal of Asian Studies*. 44:2 (February 1985).

Race, Jeffrey. *War Comes to Long An: Revolutionary Conflict in a Vietnamese Province*. Berkeley: University of California Press, 1972.

Rosen, Stephen Peter. "Vietnam and the American Theory of Limited War." *International Security* 7 (Fall 1982).

Sacks, I. Milton. "Restructuring Government in South Vietnam." *Asian Survey* (August 1967).

Salisbury, Harrison E., editor. *Vietnam Reconsidered: Lessons from a War*, New York: Harper and Row, 1984.

Schandler, Herbert Y. *The Unmaking of a President: Lyndon Johnson and Vietnam*. Princeton, N.J.: Princeton University Press, 1977.

Schlesinger, Arthur, Jr. *Bitter Heritage: Vietnam and American Democracy, 1941–1966*. Boston: Houghton Mifflin, 1968.

Schlight, John, editor. *Second Indochina War Symposium: Papers and Commentary*. Washington, D.C.: Center of Military History, United States Army, 1986.

Shaplen, Robert. "Letter From Saigon." *The New Yorker* (January 31, 1970).

———. *The Road from War: Vietnam 1965–1970*. New York: Harper and Row, 1970.

———. "Letter from Vietnam." *The New Yorker* (June 24, 1972).

Sharp, Ulysses S. Grant. *Strategy for Defeat*: Vietnam in Retrospect. San Raphael, Cal.: Presidio Press, 1978.

Stanton, Shelby L. *The Rise and Fall of an American Army. U.S. Ground Forces in Vietnam, 1965–1973*. Novato, Cal.: Presidio Press, 1985.

Stuckey, John D., and Joseph H. Pistorius. "Mobilization for the Vietnam War: A Political and Military Catastrophe." *Parameters* 15 (Spring 1985).

Summers, Harry G., Jr. *On Strategy: The Vietnam War in Context*. Novato, Cal.: Presidio Press, 1982.

————. "Palmer, Karnow, and Herrington: A Review of Recent Vietnam War Historians." *Parameters* 15 (Spring 1985).

Thayer, Thomas C. *War Without Fronts: The American Experience in Vietnam.* Boulder, Colo.: Westview Press, 1985.

Thies, Wallace J. *When Governments Collide: Operations and Diplomacy in the Vietnam Conflict, 1964–1968.* Berkeley: University of California Press, 1980.

Tho, Tran Dinh. *Pacification.* Indochina Monographs. Washington D.C.: U.S. Army Center of Military History, 1980.

Thompson, James Clay. *Rolling Thunder: Understanding Policy and Program Failure.* Chapel Hill: University of North Carolina Press, 1980.

Thompson, Sir Robert. *Revolutionary War in World Strategy, 1945–1969.* New York: Taplinger Publishing Co., 1970.

Thompson, W. Scott, and Donald D. Frizzell, editors. *The Lessons of Vietnam.* New York: Crane, Russak & Co., 1977.

Toai, Doan Van, and David Chanoff. *The Vietnamese Gulag.* New York: Simon and Schuster, 1986.

Turley, William S. *The Second Indochina War: A Short Political and Military History, 1954–1975.* Boulder, Colo.: Westview Press, 1986.

Truong, Nhu Tang. *A Vietcong Memoir.* San Diego, Cal.: Harcourt, Brace, Jovanovich, 1985.

Tzu, Sun. *The Art of War.* Edited by Samuel B. Griffith. Reprint. London: Oxford University Press, 1977.

————. *The Art of War.* Edited by James Clavell. Reprint. New York: Delacorte Press, 1983.

U.S. Department of Defense. *United States–Vietnam Relations 1945–1967.* IV.c.7.(a), Vol. I, "The Air War In North Vietnam," Washington, D.C.: U.S. Government Printing Office, 1971 (The Pentagon Papers).

Veninga, James F., and Harry A. Wilmer, editors. *Vietnam in Remission.* College Station, Tex.: Texas A&M Press, 1985.

Vien, Cao Van. *The Final Collapse.* Indochina Monographs. Washington, D.C.: U.S. Army Center of Military History, 1982.

Vien, Cao Van, and Dong Van Khuyen. *Reflections on the Vietnam War.* Indochina Monographs. Washington, D.C.: U.S. Army Center of Military History, 1980.

Walt, Lewis W. *Strange War, Strange Strategy.* New York: Funk & Wagnalls, 1970.

Westmoreland, William C., General, USA, and Ulysses S. Grant Sharp, Admiral, USN. *Report on the War in Vietnam as of 30 June 1968.* Washington, D.C.: USGPO, 1969.

Westmoreland, William. *A Soldier Reports.* Garden City, N.Y.: Doubleday and Company, 1976.

Index

About the Contributors

DR. JOE P. DUNN is Associate Professor of History and Politics, and Director of Summer Programs at Converse College, Spartanburg, SC. Of his more than twenty published articles, nine on Vietnam, particularly on historiography and teaching the war, have appeared in such journals as *Parameters, Air University Review, Naval War College Review, Armed Forces and Society, Social Studies,* and *Teaching History.* He has taught a complete course on the Vietnam War since 1974.

DR. PETER M. DUNN is a retired Air Force Colonel who served three tours in Vietnam, including 150 combat missions over North Vietnam and Laos. He was born and raised in India and schooled in the Himalayas. He holds two MAs, and a Ph.D. from the School of Oriental and African Studies, University of London. He has published extensively on the Vietnam War and on counterinsurgency and national security affairs, and in 1985 published *The First Vietnam War,* released simultaneously in Great Britain and the United States. He is currently doing post-doctoral work at the University of Missouri, Columbia, where he is an Adjunct Professor of History.

DR. NOEL C. EGGLESTON received his B.A. from Rollins College and his M.A., Ph.D. from the University of Georgia. He is Associate Professor of History at Radford University in Radford, Virginia. His dissertation investigated the roots of America's commitment in Vietnam during the Roosevelt and Truman administrations. He has also presented papers and published articles on various diplomatic and military aspects of the war and currently teaches a course on Vietnam at Radford University.

DR. LAWRENCE E. GRINTER is Professor of Asian Studies at the Air University. Montgomery, Alabama. He has a Ph.D. from the University of North

Carolina, Chapel Hill, is coeditor of three books, author of twenty published scholarly articles and reviews, and author of a dozen government studies on Asian security problems. Dr. Grinter worked in South Vietnam in on the pacification program. 1966–67. He teaches Asian security affairs and international politics at the Air University.

DR. ALAN L. GROPMAN is a principal analyst for the SYSCON Corporation of Washington, D.C. In this capacity he assists SYSCON's clients by developing war games and other simulations to improve military planning and operational effectiveness. Dr. Gropman retired from the United States Air Force as a Colonel with more than 27 years commissioned service. As a navigator he accumulated more than 4000 flying hours including more than 650 missions in Vietnam, earning him the Distinguished Flying Cross and six Air Medals, among other combat decorations. He holds a Ph.D. in military history and has taught at the United States Air Force Academy and the National War College.

DR. NGUYEN MANH HUNG received his Ph.D. in International Relations from the University of Virginia in 1965, he followed that up with study at the School of Law of the University of Saigon. He was Professor of International Politics at the National School of Administration in the Republic of Vietnam, and then Deputy-Minister of National Planning and Development. He has written numerous papers, articles, and books in both Vietnamese and English, and is currently Associate Professor of Government and Director of the Indochina Institute at George Mason University.

COLONEL HARRY G. SUMMERS, JR., U.S. Army (retired) is the senior military correspondent of the *U. S. News and World Report*. He formerly held the General Douglas MacArthur Chair of Military Research at the Army War College. A combat infantry veteran of the Korean and Vietnam wars, Colonel Summers' award-winning book, *On Strategy: A Critical Analysis of the Vietnam War*, is used as a student text by the Army, Navy, Air Force War Colleges as well as by many major civilian universities. His most recent work, the *Vietnam War Almanac*, was voted one of the outstanding source books for 1985 by the American Libraries Association.

MAJOR EARL H. TILFORD, JR., served in Southeast Asia as an intelligence officer. He holds a B.A. and M.A. from the University of Alabama and a Ph.D. in Military History from George Washington University. Major Tilford is the author of a book on Air Force search and rescue operations during the Vietnam War and has published over a dozen articles in various journals. He teaches a military history for the University of Alabama and has appeared as a guest lecturer on the Vietnam War at the University of Georgia, Pembroke State University, the University of Missouri, and Converse College. Major Tilford lives in Prattville, Alabama with his wife, three children, three cats, and a hamster.

COLONEL JOHN D. WAGHELSTEIN is Director of Theater Operations, Department of Military Strategy, Army War College. He recently commanded the 7th Special Forces Group (Airborne) Fort Bragg, North Carolina. Commissioned as an Infantry Officer, Colonel Waghelstein's overseas assignments have included two tours in Vietnam, (one with the Special Foreces, the other with 173rd Airborne Brigade) three in Panama, and other assignments in Bolivia and El Salvador. He will soon complete his Ph.D at Kansas University, and has authored articles in a variety of journals.